Response to *20/20 Money*

"Joe is someone whose passion to see you succeed is unmistakable. He cares not just about your financial health, but your future hopes and dreams that can be born out of it. In *20/20 Money*, Joe is dedicated to leading you to life-changing clarity around your future."
-- Carey Nieuwhof, Best-selling Author and Founding Pastor, Connexus Church
(Barrie, Ontario)

"Joe Sangl has spent a lifetime helping people understand how to manage the resources they have. In this new work, he encourages each of us to dream big dreams again and to believe that we will have and can manage the provision to make it happen. Get ready to start dreaming again!
-- Bishop Walter Scott Thomas, Presiding Prelate of Kingdom Association of Covenant Pastors, Pastor of New Psalmist Baptist Church
(Baltimore, MD)

"Joseph Sangl is an insightful guide on money matters. His principles can literally save you a lifetime of heartache. Read this book and live it and you will set your financial future up in a powerful way. Your future self will thank you!"
-- Pastor Jud Wilhite, Senior Pastor of Central Church
(Henderson, Nevada)

"Joe Sangl is a dreamer! The only way we can ever live our biggest dream is to find a way to fund our God-given dream. His new book, *20/20 Money*, is solid gold. It helps us move toward living a fully funded life while being crystal clear on the greatest use of the money that God has given to each of us. *20/20 Money* should be recommended reading for anyone who believes in setting goals and achieving more in life!"
-- Dr. Dwight "Ike" Reighard, author and leadership expert, President and CEO of MUST Ministries, Senior Pastor of Piedmont Church
(Marietta, Georgia)

"*20/20 Money* is a gift to anyone who wants to gain clarity for their financial future! Joseph Sangl packages wisdom-filled principles in hope-filled practical advice. No matter where you are on your financial journey, this book will benefit your life! Buy one for you and one for someone you want to see win with money."
-- Pastor J. R. Lee, Lead Pastor of Freedom Church
(Acworth, Georgia)

"The Bible says that 'a dream comes through the multitude of business' (Eccl. 5:3). In *20/20 Money*, Joe Sangl gives practical and yet biblical steps to making one's dream a reality. Over the years, I have counseled and encouraged many people with ambitious vision and faith-filled dreams that never materialized. Joe helps his readers know that it can happen and your dream can be fully funded as we do the natural work, taking clear and precise steps while God's does the supernatural work. You can live a 'fully funded life.'"
-- Bishop Dr. Herbert Bailey, Presiding Bishop of the Right Direction Fellowship, Senior Pastor of Right Direction Church International (Columbia, South Carolina)

"Joe Sangl approaches an all-important topic from such a place of wisdom and experience. I have never met anyone who shares on the subject of financial freedom with more passion than Joe. Not just financial freedom for its own sake, but for what financial freedom means to people desiring to pursue all that God has for them. I highly recommend this book for anyone who wishes to see their God-given dreams become a reality."
-- Pastor Jesse Eisenhart, Senior Pastor of True North Church (Sewell, New Jersey)

"The experts agree, the *'why'* is more important than the *'how'*, and Joe Sangl certainly demonstrates that truth in his latest book, *20/20 Money*. There's no shortage of books and tools available to help us learn how to manage our finances, get out of debt, study proven methods to save or invest - but most of them overlook the most important aspect of all: *why do we want more money?* Joe helps us answer the *'why'* question by helping us to look inside at the *dream* that God has placed within us - even if we have never shared it with anyone. Best of all, he walks us through simple explanations and practical tips as to how we can achieve those dreams by having a Fully Funded Life. Many of us haven't been motivated to practice the *how-to's* we have learned because we didn't connect them to the *why's*. *20/20 Money* provides that necessary motivation."
-- Pastor Jerry McQuay, Senior Pastor of Christian Life Center (Tinley Park, Illinois)

"Not only is Joe the most inspirational and encouraging communicator on winning with money I've ever heard, but he also does the same on paper. In *20/20 Money*, Joe takes the nuts and bolts of money management and goes one step further, walking you through the exhilarating process of identifying and funding your dreams. This is the book on money that most people don't realize how much they need."
-- Pastor Jeff Maness, Lead Pastor of Element Church
(Cheyenne, Wyoming)

"With insight that comes from experience, Joe Sangl delivers a much needed "Fire You Up" guide to your financial future. What I love about this book is that it not only captures the "WHY you need a vision for your money"" and "WHAT needs to happen," but that it also gives you a HOW. For years, Joe has been guiding many with financial wisdom, and this latest work will be the catalytic playbook for so many more."
-- Pastor Marty Schmidt, Lead Pastor of The Bridge Church
(Ottumwa, Iowa)

"A blank sheet of paper will drain the energy out of a room full of leaders. A page full of ideas, dreams and ideas will bring untold amounts of motivation and fuel to move forward. *20/20 Money* is a powerful guide to empower you to ink your vision and realize God's redemptive dreams for your life."
-- Rev. Dr. Charles Kyker, Senior Pastor of Christ Church
(Hickory, North Carolina)

"Joe Sangl has done it again! His new book, *20/20 Money,* is like a visit to the eye doctor, it will help you gain "clarity" on how to get where you have always wanted to go! What a blessing Joe is to those that are chasing their dreams and trying to fund them!"
-- Pastor Mike Linch, Host of Linch with a Leader Podcast and Senior Pastor of NorthStar Church
(Kennesaw, Georgia)

20/20 Money

Gaining Clarity for your Financial Future

20/20 Money: Gaining Clarity for your Financial Future
Published in the United States of America by NIN Publishing – Anderson, SC

Printed in the United States of America
Signature Book Printing, www.sbpbooks.com

Cover design by Megan Hibbard
Edited by Rachel Rivers

Library of Congress Control Number: 2019951727

Sangl, Joseph

ISBN: 978-0-578-58749-3

First Edition

To my bride, Jennifer, and our children: Melea, Keaton, and Megan.

It is a *joy* to chase dreams together!

CONTENTS

Introduction

I have yet to meet a person who doesn't enjoy talking about a dream. Because of the opportunities afforded me to teach about personal finances, I have had the privilege to speak with many people about their dreams. Whether it is a personal hope or one for his or her children or grandchildren, close friends, or even the world itself, there is a certain spark that appears in the eyes of those who have clear dreams.

In 2004, I began this journey to help people win with their money. It is my desire to help people accomplish far more than they ever thought possible with their personal finances. It is fueled by a core belief that when people are financially free, they are much more likely to do *exactly* what they have been put on earth to do — regardless of the cost or income potential. After nearly two decades of pursuing this vision, my passion hasn't waned at all. In fact, it's only grown clearer and stronger.

Many people believe I am most excited about helping others become debt free or begin to invest. While it is true that such financial success energizes me, my real exuberance is driven by what I know is going to happen as a result of their financial improvements. Because of their focused effort, a family is going to fight less about money. A marriage can be restored and strengthened. Children will be equipped with financial tools and principles that will help them avoid painful money mistakes. Families are going to be able to live generously and pursue a Fully Funded Life. Dream trips can become realities. College educations will be funded. People will be able to position themselves to leave an inheritance and legacy for their children's children.

Most of the resources we have created over the past 15 years have focused on helping people manage their money. However, something that has stood out to me over the past several years is just how many people feel stuck in their financial journeys. Because of this, they find it difficult to even allow themselves to dream. It is apparent that people need help with learning how to dream again and assistance in connecting those dreams to their dollars.

One of the top reasons people seize up when it comes to dreaming is because they recognize the extraordinary costs involved. They instinctively know their regular income will never be able to fund many of their big dreams. After an exhausting attempt to think of alternative ways to raise the money necessary to fund them, most people just give up on their dreams.

There have been many books written about finding purpose and chasing dreams. Most of them lack practical instruction on determining ways to fund those dreams. There have been many other books focused on helping people win with their money. Most of these make an assumption that people already have taken appropriate amounts of time to think through their God-given plans, hopes, and dreams.

My hope with this book is to provide instruction on both. It will help you gain 20/20 vision for your life while also obtaining 20/20 clarity for how each plan, hope, and dream will be funded. We call it *20/20 Money: Gaining Clarity for Your Financial Future*. It is my prayer that this resource will be a catalyst that propels you toward a Fully Funded Life!

1

A DREAM SETS YOUR EYES AGLEAM

"What are your plans, hopes, and dreams?" This is a question I always ask at the Financial Learning Experience, a two-hour financial education event I teach throughout the country. It is always one of my favorite moments because the question energizes the entire room. After all, who doesn't like to dream about the future?

Then I ask people to respond to a quick follow-up question: "Raise your hand if you do not have your plans, hopes, and dreams *written down.*" Typically, more than half of the people raise their hands.

It's the same at every single event. People are energized by the dream question and challenged by the action required. Even though I have taught hundreds of these events, I'm still blown away by the number of people who have not taken the time and energy to write down their dreams.

We each receive one life to live. One. Isn't it worth taking the time to dream a little? After all, it is a dream that sets the eyes agleam! It sparks an unquenchable fire—and even though it energizes and instills passion in a person like nothing else, more than half of us haven't even taken the time to write down our plans, hopes, and dreams. Of course, just because they aren't written down doesn't mean a person is without dreams, but there is something powerful about putting pen to paper.

The day you write your dreams down, something will solidify within you. It will galvanize your dreams. It is a step of great faith because in the very instant you choose to write the dream, it means you desire it enough to at least put it on paper. You will have taken a step of faith to really believe it could become a reality and developed enough trust to allow others to potentially see and know your dream.

Do *you* have your plans, hopes, and dreams written down? This is the number one reason people fail in their financial journeys. They don't truly know what is at stake. They haven't taken the time to write down their plans, hopes, and dreams. As a result, they don't understand the direct connection between their financial decisions and their dreams.

Every single dream will cost money—directly or indirectly. It is my passion to help you achieve them. I call this living a Fully Funded Life which I define as "being able to do exactly what you have been put on earth to do—regardless of the cost or income potential."

> **Fully Funded Life**: Being able to do exactly what you have been put on earth to do – regardless of the cost or income potential.

Without clarity for your plans, hopes, and dreams—your Fully Funded Life—you will be susceptible to wander your way through life—especially financially. Oprah referenced this exact way of living in her Debt Diet series. In this program, she talked about the importance of understanding why we behave in a certain way when she stated, "Way too many of us are walking through life unconsciously."[i]

When considering the vision for your life, think about examples you can see all around you. Have you ever attempted to drive a car with a fogged-up windshield? It is impossible to move safely without clarity. When you turn on the defog fan, isn't it wonderful to watch the fog just go away? When you choose to write down your plans, hopes, and dreams, it is similar to turning on the defog fan. You begin to gain a newfound clarity for your life.

If you have found yourself continually stuck in the spin-cycle of preparing a budget and then failing to follow it, becoming frustrated, then preparing a new budget only to ignore it too—I would encourage you to take one step back in your financial planning and set aside some time to write down all of your plans, hopes, and dreams. These dreams will provide clarity of vision for all of your subsequent financial decisions. For many people, it is as if the fog suddenly lifts from their vision, and they see their money in a completely new light.

The dream sets your eyes agleam. How long has it been since you enthusiastically approached your life and dreams? If you've been unconsciously going through the motions, it's time to see the power that dreams have on your ability to stick to the financial decisions and systems that will help you fund them.

One of the greatest songs ever written is *Amazing Grace*. Let's take a look at the lyrics of the first verse.

Amazing Grace! How sweet the sound,
That saved a wretch; like me!
I once was lost, but now am found,
Was blind, but now I see.

This song is talking about the miracle of salvation, and the words and chords make it one of my favorite songs to play on the piano. I have played this song at least a thousand times. Through the wisdom I have gained over the years, I have seen the profound truth of these words in all areas of my life, including my financial journey.

There was a day when I was lost, financially. There were many years where I was blind — having no vision at all — as to how I could address my money situation.

Then a day came when I awakened from my wandering. My pivotal moment came when my friend, Tim, asked me a question: "If you had one million dollars, what would you do?" For the first time in my life, I truly understood the point of the question. It wasn't really so much about the money as it was about the vision I had for my life. It was about the plans, hopes, and dreams that were yet unfulfilled. It was about thinking beyond the daily busyness of life and truly considering what life could be in the future.

There was just one problem with Tim's question; I couldn't answer it. In fact, it was more than three years later when I had a breakthrough that finally provided some clarity for my future — and an answer to Tim's question. It happened during a flight on a Southwest Airlines Boeing 737. I had settled into my normal window seat in the back of the plane. It was time for another four-hour flight from San Diego to Chicago. At the time, I was providing engineering and leadership support for the launch of a new manufacturing line in Tijuana, Mexico, and this flight had become a normal part of my life.

For some reason on this flight, I began to write down all of my plans, hopes, and dreams. The flight went by very quickly because I was so focused on writing. The pen seemed to be alive in my hands as dreams poured out of it onto the paper. I thought about the places Jenn and I wanted to visit, the life we wanted to live, our dreams for our daughter and future children, and organizations we wanted to support with our time and money.

As the flight prepared for landing, I looked over all of the dreams on the paper and asked myself the question, "If we keep managing money the way we are right now, will we be able to accomplish all of this?" I was not happy with my response! While it wasn't a good feeling at the time, it sparked a fire in me that helped power my family to make real and lasting changes to our financial behavior.

An ordinary airplane ride turned into an extraordinary life-changing event! That very instant, I began to really dream of what my life could be. My eyes were agleam! Because of this, Jenn and I began to think differently about the future. We continued writing down additional things we wanted to accomplish with our lives — individually and together as a family.

Of course, we had dreams before this moment. The difference now was that these dreams were clear and written down. We took the time to think through each one. As time went by, we thought of new things to add to our dreams list. In addition, this process generated something even more powerful: belief that our dreams could come true. We now *knew* our dreams could actually become a reality.

Many people make the same mistake. We were allowing our bank account balance to dictate whether or not our dreams could actually become reality. Let me tell you this: when your average bank account balance is hovering around $4.13 and you're allowing it to determine your future plans, hopes, and dreams, you won't have very big dreams — if any at all!

Our newfound dreams set our eyes agleam.

Do you have your plans, hopes, and dreams written down? Have your eyes been lit up with the fire generated by a clear vision for your future?

It's time! You only have one life. It's time to think beyond your bank account balance. Consider what could happen in the rest of your days if you began to truly dream. It can be easy to make excuses. "We're broke." "We're too old to chase a dream." "I've failed in the past. Why would this be any different?" "I'll dream again once I get these children raised and out of the house." "My friends and family tell me I'm crazy."

Instead of believing and repeating lies like these, stop the excuses and start dreaming again. Refuse to exchange the truth for a lie. You *can* dream. You *can* experience a Fully Funded Life. Dr. John C. Maxwell shared in his great book, *Put Your Dream to the Test*, that one of the wonderful things about dreaming is "…in the beginning, dreams are free!"

Here's something I find amazing about dreaming. Kids have no problem with it. They shoot for the stars. From time to time, I have the opportunity to teach kids some basic personal finance topics. As I always do, I start by addressing their dreams. When asked what their dreams are, the answers pour out. The classroom usually descends into sheer pandemonium as they share their hopes for the future. Many want to be star athletes. Others want to be princesses. They want to travel the world. In their dreams, all of them have a nice home, a great car, and perfect children.

Invariably, the adults in the room begin to look at each other with knowing smiles mixed with hints of cynicism. Why? Because adults understand the cost side of the dream equation. They have experienced the heartache of disappointment. It's almost as if they want to pat each child on the head and say, "Just you wait and see. Most of those dreams are never going to come true."

It's true. Some of their dreams will not come true. However, if they don't pursue them, *none* of them will! Isn't life worth writing down your plans, hopes, and dreams so that you might achieve *something* versus *nothing*?

Here's the point: Children have no problem believing. As adults, we have no problem disbelieving. When it comes to something as important as dreaming, let's be more like kids!

> Children have no problem believing.
> As adults, we have no problem disbelieving.

Of course, no one dreams of challenging curveballs like divorce, sickness, premature death of a loved one, a wayward child, a bankrupt business, or a career failure. When something like this happens in your life, it is up to you whether or not the challenge will cause you to give up and stop dreaming or if you will utilize it to learn and push forward.

You are in control of far more of your life than you may believe. Are you out of shape? You can start a new diet and exercise plan today. Do you lack education on a topic? You can sign up for a class or watch YouTube videos on the topic right now! Are you dealing with a broken relationship? You can pick up the phone or drive to their house immediately and initiate a much-needed conversation. At the very least, you can choose to forgive them right now. Do you want to a make a difference in the world? Sign up to volunteer with a local service project right now. Are your kids out of control? You can establish new boundaries this very instant and begin to enforce them.

There are many complexities to life, to be sure, but so many of life's challenges persist simply because someone has chosen to operate in the position of victim instead of choosing to take responsibility and make decisions that would address and improve the situation. It's time to make decisions, financial and otherwise, that help propel you toward your plans, hopes, and dreams.

There are, of course, many books that focus on helping you define your dreams and provide ways to help pursue them. However, a dream without money will remain a dream. There are many other resources that focus on helping you win with money. My goal with this book is to help you connect the two.

This is the entire premise of this book: I believe you can live a Fully Funded Life. It starts with having 20/20 vision of your future. When you begin to dream again and make better financial decisions, it will help you move toward the preferred vision you have for your life—a Fully Funded Life.

A Dream Sets Your Eyes Agleam

At some time, you've probably visited an optometrist to assess the current state of your vision. The doctor had you look at an eye chart and asked you to read lines of letters that systematically reduced in size. They use this test to determine your current ability to see. If there is a deficiency, the doctor will then have you look through a variety of lenses and ask which ones allow you to see better, "Number 1 or Number 2?" After hearing your response and making another adjustment to the lenses, the doctor asks the question again saying, "Number 3 or Number 4?" Once they have determined the best lens combination, they can usually provide a prescription that allows you to see with perfect vision. The eye doctor calls this 20/20 vision.

In this book, we will look at your future using a variety of lenses so you can begin to clearly see with perfect 20/20 vision and move rapidly toward living a Fully Funded Life.

2

CRYSTAL CLEAR

When I was a kid, the highlight of every summer was an opportunity to attend church camp. About 400 children from all over the state would descend on the campground for their assigned week of camp. One of the main focuses of camp was the kid's choir. Participation was mandatory. Each morning, we were required to gather together to learn a new song that we would sing in the nightly church service. While I'm sure many kids were disappointed to have their other activities interrupted, I actually enjoyed choir practice because I love music — especially the type of gospel music we were singing which featured the Hammond B3 organ.

Each morning, the camp choir director would have all the kids move up into the large choir loft at the front of the tabernacle so we could practice our singing in preparation for the evening service. One year, when I was around twelve years old, I was walking up to the front of the church and noticed a large blank white banner that stretched across the entire platform. As I got closer to the choir loft, I realized the banner had huge letters printed on it, spelling out the camp's theme for the week. I had discovered a massive issue: I lacked clear vision.

A few weeks later, a visit to the optometrist revealed my nearsightedness and astigmatism and a pair of eyeglasses were ordered for me. I'll never forget the day I put on my first pair of glasses. I could see. I could really see! As I looked out of the eye doctor's office, I could see a McDonald's across the street. There were some trees out in front of it. I could actually see the individual leaves fluttering in the breeze. I looked down at the carpet, and I could see each individual carpet fiber. I could see!

Do you desire this type of clarity for your life? Do you know where you want to go in the future? Do you know where you want to live? What about the possessions you would like to have? What type of lifestyle do you want to experience? What causes do you want to support with your time and money?

You will never forget when you gain 20/20 clarity for your life. Just as it happened when I received my first pair of glasses, you will feel like the entire world has changed and opened up for you.

I talk a lot about living a Fully Funded Life — being able to do exactly what you've been put on earth to do regardless of the cost or income potential. What does a Fully Funded Life look like for you? What does it *really* look like?

This is a crucial question. If you don't know the answer, it is time to get some "glasses" to help you see more clearly. My hope is that this book will help you in the same way my visit to the optometrist changed my life.

Without clarity for your Fully Funded Life, it is difficult to make progress — especially in your finances. Everyone *knows* they would benefit greatly if they prepared and followed a budget each and every month, but the majority of people *don't* prepare a one. One of the surveys conducted by the I Was Broke. Now I'm Not.

team revealed that 62.5% of respondents do not employ this simple, but powerful, financial tool.

Why would the majority of people choose not to utilize this valuable tool? I submit that one of the biggest reasons is because they are not crystal clear on what a Fully Funded Life looks like for them. They haven't taken the time to really consider what their life could look like. They lack clarity – and without clarity it is difficult to prepare a budget and stick to it.

Preparing a budget just because it is a good idea rarely provides the fuel for a person to continue the habit. However, when someone knows where she is headed with her life, when it is crystal clear, then she knows *why* it is worth going through the challenges of preparing and living by a monthly budget. When faced with a challenging financial decision, you can view it through the lens of how it will affect progress toward your Fully Funded Life.

Are you beginning to understand the value of clarity? Do you *see* it?

Helen Keller was an author, speaker, political activist, and lecturer. She was also blind and deaf. In spite of her challenges, she became the first deaf-blind person to earn a Bachelor of Arts degree. She is credited with saying, "The only thing worse than being blind is having sight but no vision." What a powerful statement. It is true for your life too. Have you clarified the vision for your life, or are you wandering around, stuck and playing the role of victim? Are things happening to you or are you happening to things around you? Are you regressing or progressing? It is time to clarify the vision for your future so that you don't waste any part of your one and only life.

When a person has a crystal-clear vision of their plans, hopes, and dreams, it generates within them a great energy and passion. It helps them make the otherwise challenging and difficult decisions that stall a person who has no vision. Your vision of a Fully Funded Life will power you through obstacles that would have previously stopped you in your tracks.

A 20/20 vision of your future can be described many ways, but here are three words to think about: crisp, clear, and compelling.

Crisp

You should be able to quickly describe what a Fully Funded Life looks like for you. Of course, each dream has layers of depth you could spend hours talking about. However, as you work to define your plans, hopes, and dreams through this book, it is my hope that you will be able to summarize your Fully Funded Life into one or two statements.

Clear

As you talk about your Fully Funded Life, it should be clear to you and those you love what your preferred future looks like. This clarity will help you swiftly make decisions on opportunities that arise from time to time. You will be able to ask, "Will this opportunity move me toward my Fully Funded Life?" Clarity will allow you to give an answer immediately.

Compelling

Your Fully Funded Life should be attractive and interesting to you, even if it will require a lot of hard work. This is actually a great way to determine whether or not you are pursuing someone else's dream for your life. You will quickly grow weary of talking about a dream someone else has for you. However, you will feel compelled to talk about your dream for years to come. You will never tire of talking about or pursuing it.

As you ponder the challenging questions that lie ahead in this book, remember you are seeking to gain a crisp, clear, and compelling vision for a Fully Funded Life. You will have to fight for it. Clarity requires constant defense. Life has a way of throwing continual distractions your way. Many of them will be good things, but as you look at them through the proper lens, you will determine that some of them, while good, will actually inhibit or prevent you from making progress toward your preferred future.

Before we dive into defining your Fully Funded Life, it is important to further understand some of the consequences of having an unclear vision. This will be addressed in the upcoming chapter.

3

CONSEQUENCES OF UNCLEAR VISION

Basketball is my favorite sport. As I was growing up alongside my five brothers, my father built a basketball court for us. He installed a six-by-six-inch post into the ground, cut out a plywood backboard, and put a rim and net up for us. With six boys who all loved basketball, there was no chance for any grass to grow because we wore that area out all year long. As a teenager, I would join my friends in playing hours of basketball after church. We played anywhere there was a basketball goal available, including the local Boy's Club and its adjacent park. Invariably, after our weeknight church service, our favorite thing to do was go to the park and play basketball. There was just one problem: the lights were turned off! It's hard to play basketball in the dark.

As mischievous teenagers, it didn't take long for us to discover that the timer controlling the lights was attached to a power pole about fifteen feet above the ground. Two boys would be assigned to climb the pole and adjust the timer so the lights would turn on. The rest of us would run toward the court to start shooting around as the metal-halide lights warmed up.

On one particular night, I was running to the court in total darkness and ran straight into a two-foot tall post, made from an old telephone pole, that had been installed to keep cars out of the grassy areas of the park. I never saw it coming. As the lights slowly brightened, it revealed me writhing on the ground in miserable agony and pain, praying I hadn't broken my leg. Luckily, my shin was just terribly bruised, but I was sidelined from playing basketball for a couple of weeks. Running without clear vision left me hurt and unable to do what I loved to do.

Unclear vision makes it hard to get back up.

This is exactly what happens to many people in their financial journey. They are running in the darkness without clear vision for their Fully Funded Life. From time to time, financial events occur that knock them down. It's hard to muster up the courage to get back up to pursue a goal that isn't clear.

A person without clear vision is highly susceptible to be drawn to the passions of an individual who has clarity for his own Fully Funded Life. It is like the visionless person has an internal vacuum drawing them toward the energy and passion of other people, and in this process, he will mistakenly try to adopt the other person's vision.

Don't make this mistake! It is, of course, important to have mentors and heroes who help inspire you to greatness, but be true to who you are and your individual plans, hopes, and dreams.

Unclear vision can cause you to feel overwhelmed.

In one survey conducted by the I Was Broke. Now I'm Not. team, 927 people responded. One of the questions was, "If you were given $1,000,000 right now, what would you do with it?" It was amazing to see how many people couldn't even begin to fathom what to do. One respondent perhaps summarized these feelings best when she wrote: "Don't know. That is too much money for me to understand how best to use it."

Of the hundreds of respondents, very few were able to clearly articulate what they would do with the money. I suspect you already know why. They lack clarity on what their Fully Funded Life looks like. As a result, the question overwhelms them.

The opposite is also true. With 20/20 vision, you will be able to rattle off exactly how to use the money. It won't be overwhelming at all. In fact, because you've taken time to consider, think, and pray about your plans, hopes, and dreams and because you have written them down, your response will almost be instinctive!

Unclear vision leads to a lot of wandering.

Have you worked for a person who constantly switches things up? They assign you to a task, only to assign you to do something else right as you began to work on the first one. It can drive you crazy, right?

Why would a leader consistently do this to his team? It probably isn't because he is a bad person or trying to frustrate people. It's likely due to a lack of clear vision. It's called being double-minded. The Bible actually references this in James1:8: "Such a person is double-minded and unstable in all they do." This passage is written about a person who lacks wisdom and doubts their next steps. Does this sound similar to anyone you know?

There's only one thing worse than working for or living with a person like this: it is *being* a person like this! If you don't have a clear vision for your future, you will be just like the double-minded person. Your focus will be all over the place. It will feel like your brain is scrambled eggs. I have experienced this in my own life, and it is not a pleasant feeling. The entire earth below your feet feels like quicksand without hope of solid ground.

Unclear vision directly impacts your money decisions. Without a clear understanding of one's preferred future, it is very difficult to stick to tough financial decisions. You won't be able to prioritize your focus long enough to make substantial progress. One day, you will be fired up about preparing and following a budget so you can save money to start a business. The next day, you will be justifying why it was okay to spend money on an item that totally derailed the business dream.

To be sure, money can be quite confusing. We want to save money, but we also want to pay off debt. We know we need to invest for retirement, but we want to go on vacation and enjoy life right now. It is our desire to live generously, but how can anyone do that with all of the bills and debts facing us? Then there is the challenge of raising kids and helping them with college. Let's not even talk about purchasing and paying off a house!

Do you feel the tension? Without clear vision, it is so easy to just fall into the abyss and wander around for ten or twenty years without making any progress at all—financial or otherwise!

Confusion, frustration, depression, and anger can invade your life.

Have you ever met a person who is continually confused, frustrated, depressed, or angry? There is a high probability she doesn't have 20/20 direction for her life. An aimless person will have no focused outlet for these negative emotions, so they strike out in every direction. Without a clear target, she will struggle to manage her emotions in a way that propels her forward.

Pursuing a Fully Funded Life will provide its fair share of confusion, disappointment, frustration, and anger, but there is a difference between how these emotions are navigated based upon vision clarity. A person with a complete understanding of his Fully Funded Life is able to utilize these feelings as fuel to move toward his dreams. It allows him to become more resolute in achieving goals. A person without clear direction will be prone to become overwhelmed and surrender to his feelings.

One of the greatest ways to prevent these emotions from ruling your life is to have 20/20 vision. When the vision is crystal clear, it provides a great outlet for negative emotions. The power of seeing a dream being accomplished in the future will help you persevere until a breakthrough is experienced.

Unclear vision makes a person susceptible to believing and repeating a lie.

When a person has an unclear vision for her life, it can make her vulnerable to believing lies. Have you ever met someone who possessed great talent, yet didn't believe she really had any skill at all? There is a good chance she was believing a lie told by someone else. It is easy for lazy people who have no vision for their own lives to be intimidated or challenged by someone who is fired up about pursuing his own Fully Funded Life. A favorite statement uttered by visionless people is this: "You'll never amount to anything." They also like to say, "When you fail, don't come whining about it to me."

Without 20/20 vision, you might mistakenly choose to share a new dream with someone who is unable to handle it. Without the passion, commitment, and energy that a crystal-clear vision provides, it is almost like entrusting your baby to the care of a lion! When negative people react to your dream by immediately tearing it apart, it is like they have harmed your baby. It is a very painful experience.

When your vision is in process and your dream is in its infancy, be careful with whom you share your dream. At first, when your dream is still new, it is difficult enough to believe in it without having naysayers trying to tear it down. If you allow yourself to continue to hear their disparaging and discouraging words, it can become very easy to start believing them. Hang around long enough, and you'll start repeating the lies! In this type of environment, it won't be long before you give up on your dream.

Ultimately, an unclear vision will result in an experience similar to when I ran in the park in the dark. You will be going somewhere, but you will experience one painful moment after another without making much progress. The consequences of a visionless life are tremendous. Make sure you live your one and only life in a way that matters most to you — a Fully Funded Life.

4

GUIDELINES FOR CLARIFYING YOUR FULLY FUNDED LIFE

In the book of Proverbs, we find these words of wisdom: *"Where there is no revelation, people cast off restraint;"* (Proverbs 29:18) When you have no revelation (no vision) for your life, it is easy to live for the minute and make decisions that preclude you from the preferred vision you have for your life.

Let's look a little closer at this nugget of wisdom. This verse states that "without vision, people cast off restraint." This tells us what happens without 20/20 vision. Let's think about the opposite, positive side, of this scenario. What happens if there is clear revelation? I submit that people will show and even embrace restraint. I have certainly seen this to be true in my own life. In the times when I have been wandering without clarity for the future, I have cast off restraints and the results have been costly. When I have had a clear vision for the future, I was able to embrace the restraints required to achieve it.

The writings of the prophet Habakkuk appear in the Old Testament. In Habakkuk 2:2, the following statement is recorded: "…Write down the revelation and make it plain on tablets so that a herald may run with it." It is as true today as the day it was written more than 2,600 years ago. It is indeed important to write down the revelation, the God-given vision, for your life. When you write down the vision and *make it plain*, it makes it easier to run with it.

Now it is time to put in the work of determining what a Fully Funded Life looks like for you, and write the vision.

Clarifying your Fully Funded Life is going to require some challenging work so to get started, let's set some guidelines as you begin to write the vision for your life.

Guideline #1: *No one else can write the vision for you.*

This is all about you and your calling. I can't write your vision for you. Your parents or siblings might try to write it for you, but it won't be your own. Although they might have good insight into the skills and talents you possess, your friends won't do it for you either.

If you feel like you are facing a concrete wall when seeking the calling for your life, let me point you to a Scripture that has been very helpful to many. It is found in Romans 12:1-2: "¹ Therefore, I urge you, brothers and sisters, in view of God's mercy, to offer your bodies as a living sacrifice, holy and pleasing to God—this is your true and proper worship. ² Do not conform to the pattern of this world, but be transformed by the renewing of your mind. Then you will be able to test and approve what God's will is—his good, pleasing and perfect will."

As an engineer, what immediately stands out to me is that this verse reads like a piece of computer code with an "if-then" statement. There are three big "ifs" in this passage of Scripture that, when true, will allow the "then" part to be true. Do you see them? Let's review the passage again through this lens: (1) *If* you offer your body as a living sacrifice and (2) *if* you don't conform to the pattern of this world and (3) *if* you are transformed by the renewing of your mind *then* you will be able to test and approve what God's will is—his good, pleasing and perfect will.

IF you offer your body as a living sacrifice

Only you can offer your body as a living sacrifice to the Lord. Are you willing to live your life poured out for others and give up your dreams for something greater? I love the poetry of the phrase "a living sacrifice." You can *live* while being a sacrifice! It is not always easy to do, but this is a great way to choose to live your life because it is holy and pleasing to Him.

My journey to offer myself as a living sacrifice was challenging. I had to give up on my dream to become a corporate CEO. I had expended a lot of effort to position myself for the climb. Academically, I obtained a BS-Mechanical Engineering degree from Purdue University, a Master's in Business Administration from Clemson University, and I completed numerous leadership training certifications. Experientially, I accepted job transfers and relocations and traveled extensively to gain valuable business knowledge.

But I knew I was called to help people win with their money and live Fully Funded Lives. I wrestled with the decision for months. I distinctly remember the day I chose to offer my body as a living sacrifice. I was helping lead a business meeting in Salt Lake City, Utah, when I made the commitment to sacrifice my corporate dream for the opportunity to pursue my calling. It was February 22, 2006. Faced with the challenges of giving up on my own dreams to pursue an unknown future, I cried. There were many sacrifices that would be required to achieve my God-given calling, many of which I did not know or understand at the time, but I'm so glad I did it.

IF you don't conform to the pattern of this world

You must not be conformed to the pattern of this world. If you let it, the world will tell you how to live your life. People will gladly give you their opinions and thoughts. The pattern of the world will point you to more, bigger, and better. More power and position. Bigger house and income. Better car and technology. Misdirected, all of this will lead to greed, strife, envy, gossip, discontent, and selfishness. This is why we mustn't be conformed to the pattern of this world.

Giving up my corporate American dream didn't make sense to many people. I left my excellent job to take a new role with a 50% pay cut. I left a clear career path for one that was murky and unclear. Jenn and I downgraded our house and moved eleven hours away for a job without bonus opportunities or promotions available.

On the surface, it didn't make sense, but I wasn't interested in what others thought. I went through this Romans 12:1-2 process and had complete confidence in the 20/20 vision for my future. Be prepared for this: when you refuse to conform to the pattern of this world, it will get the attention of others. At first, they might scoff and scorn, but when the Fully Funded Life comes to fruition, they will take note. The doubters will begin to disappear.

IF you are transformed by the renewing of your mind

According to Dictionary.com, the word "renew" means "to begin or take up again."[ii] I love this definition! Said another way using this definition, it can be read as "be transformed by beginning to use your mind again!"

This sort of transformation takes place through prayer, reading God's Word, and seeking wise counsel. As I sought God's calling for my life, my mind was renewed. Because of this transformation, I was able to deal with people who were confused by the abandonment of my previous dreams to pursue this new calling to help people win with their money.

Seek God for clarity on your Fully Funded Life. As you do so, you will be transformed by the renewing of your mind. When this happens, you will view the world in stunning clarity — with 20/20 vision. You will be amazed at how differently you see things — your life, your calling, your family, and your surroundings. Everything will be changed.

THEN you will be able to test and approve what God's will is — his good, pleasing and perfect will.

It is wonderful when you have clarity on your calling. Defining what a Fully Funded Life looks like for you won't be difficult at all. It will be absolutely clear.

I remember when flat-screen high definition televisions arrived in stores. They were distinctly better than the existing technology. The improved clarity and resolution were instantly noticeable. It was obviously better. I wasn't the only one who noticed the vast improvement. It wasn't long before Goodwill and other thrift stores began to have a pile of CRT television sets. They are now so out-of-date that even thrift stores won't accept them as donations anymore. When you have clarity for your Fully Funded Life, it will be like seeing the future in HD for the first time. It will be crystal clear.

How does one test and approve God's good, pleasing, and perfect will? For me, the test was to jump out in faith, leaving my great job and future opportunities behind, exchanging it for his calling on my life. It came about as a direct result of offering my body as a living sacrifice; exchanging my dreams for the Lord's calling. My mind had been renewed, and I was able to test and approve his will.

My test was rewarded with a deep peace and confidence. It allowed me to confidently resign from my workplace. This deep peace provided comfort as I told my friends and family of my decision to chase a dream. As Paul wrote in Philippians 4:7, "And the peace of God, which transcends all understanding, will guard your hearts and your minds in Christ Jesus." I pray you will experience this same peace as you seek his will for your life.

Guideline #2 *Don't allow past failures to guide future dreams.*

One of the biggest errors we can make is to allow past mistakes to prevent us from dreaming of the future. After all, we have all failed at something in the past. If you have a favorite sport, how good were you the first time you attempted to play it? The first time Tiger Woods swung a golf club, it didn't result in a 350-yard shot that split the fairway, but it didn't stop him from taking another swing. He has won more than 80 professional tournaments and 15 majors in his Hall of Fame career.

Michael Jordan wasn't selected for the varsity basketball team in his sophomore year of high school.[iii] A Newsweek article shares about the time he found out he didn't make the team: "It was embarrassing not making the team," Jordan later said. He went home, locked himself in his room, and cried. Then he picked himself up and turned the cut into motivation. He went on to win six NBA Championships.

Failure is part of the path to success. Embrace the past challenges, seek to learn and grow from each one, and continue toward your Fully Funded Life. I remember when we were first starting our journey to help people win with their money. We decided to put on some regional conferences. For one of them, we rented an 1,100-seat facility. Less than 15 people showed up. It was very awkward, but it didn't stop us from regrouping and once again begin moving forward.

Guideline #3 *Don't let your bank account balance dictate your dreams to you.*

When you have a bank account with no money, it can be demoralizing. This is especially true when you are asked to share your vision for the future because you know the price required for each of your dreams. As a result, many people refuse to dream. Think about it. People tend to stop dreaming simply because they have no money. How crazy is that?

If I had chosen to allow my bank account to determine my dreams, I would have been allowed to have $4.13 worth of dreams. You can't get very far in life with that amount of money. However, because I chose to embrace the tension of writing down dreams I did not yet have the financial ability to fund, it generated the energy necessary to pursue them.

As I mentioned earlier in Chapter 1, a lack of money doesn't stop children from dreaming. Ask any child to share his or her dreams, and you are sure to receive an enthusiastic response. Some of their dreams might cost several million dollars, yet they are able to easily dream of the future. They do not allow the cost to shackle them. As adults, we tend to reverse this process. We know the state of our finances, so we just opt out of dreaming altogether.

Don't let this be you. Choose to write down all of the plans, hopes, and dreams that equal a Fully Funded Life for you — regardless of the cost or income potential. It is amazing how the process of dreaming will help you begin to change your behavior in ways that have a direct impact on your money.

Guideline #4 *Write down the vision.*

There is something powerful about writing down your plans, hopes, and dreams. A study conducted by psychologist Gail Matthews showed that when people wrote down their goals, they were 33% more successful in achieving them than those who formulated them in their heads.[iv] Perhaps this is why the prophet Habakkuk wrote, "Write the vision and make it plain…"

While it is very important to ponder in your heart what a Fully Funded Life looks like, be sure to take the next step and write down your thoughts. You will find it brings more clarity and helps you solidify your thoughts. More importantly, it is a step of faith. When you keep your dreams to yourself, safely tucked away in the corners of your mind, no one knows about them. No one.

Let me ask you an important question. In fact, I believe it is the most important question in this book. What is the big dream you've always had, but you have never told anyone about?

You know exactly the dream I am talking about. It is the dream you have had for years, maybe even decades, but you have never told a single soul about it for fear that it might never come true. You are scared that your friends and family might scorn, scoff, or outright laugh out loud at your dream, so you keep it to yourself, safely tucked away in your mind. Because of this, you've made little to no progress toward the dream becoming reality.

Tiger Woods had huge dreams for his future, and he wasn't afraid of writing them down or telling others. In fact, at the age of five years old he boldly stated, "When I'm going to be 20, I'm going to beat Jack Nicklaus and Tom Watson..."[v] What would compel such a young person to make such a bold statement? Maybe it was because he was a prodigy, or perhaps it was because he was still a child who wasn't scared of dreaming. I believe it was partly because he intuitively understood the value of having his vision known by others. For it is in the instance of sharing his dream that he could begin to feel the accountability created by his own words.

It's time to write the dream and make it plain. Take this valuable step of faith. Yes, others might see your dream. Yes, some people may laugh at it. When you take the bold step to write your dream down, you move from being a carrier of the dream to an owner of it. You will find this ownership will galvanize your vision of the future and provide energy to passionately pursue it.

> When you take the bold step to write your dream down, you move from being a carrier of the dream to an owner of it.

Guideline #5 *Review the PAST, analyze the PRESENT, and desire the FUTURE.*

We can learn a lot about ourselves by reviewing our past. In fact, it is our past actions, interactions, relationships, and money decisions that have led to our present condition. The same is true for the future. See if you agree with this thought: what a person does today will have a direct impact on his future ten years from now.

> What people do today will have a direct
> impact on their future ten years from now.

Comprehending the truth of this thought is highly important. When people understand the gravity of it, it completely changes the way they choose to live. It forces them to move from the "unconscious living" described by Oprah to pursuing life with a focused purpose.

I chose to go to Purdue University to study mechanical engineering. This singular decision affected all of my future. While I didn't know it at the time, I met my future bride the very first weekend I was on campus. I was offered free stuff in exchange for completing some credit card applications, so I filled out all of them. One of those companies approved a credit account for me and mailed me a credit card. The next day I used it and began my headlong plunge into debt. I began dating Sallie Mae, the student loan company, and this further extended my relationship with debt. I worked a full-time job every summer and held a part-time job throughout the school year to pay for my books and regular living expenses.

All of these past actions led me to where I am today. Some of my decisions were good ones while others led to undesirable consequences, and the same is true for you. Analyze where you currently are on your journey to a Fully Funded Life. What decisions and actions from the past are affecting you to this very day?

As a human, you have certainly made some mistakes along the way. The point of reviewing the past and analyzing the present is not to marinate in past regrets, poor choices, and negative events. The value of this exercise is to cement the understanding that what we do *right now* will have a direct impact on how we get to live our lives *in the future*. Learn from the past and let it inform you on changes that must be made to achieve your preferred future.

Pastor Mike Linch, the leader of NorthStar Church in Kennesaw, Georgia, experienced the value of this exercise. The church had experienced substantial growth and built several new facilities to accommodate all of the needs for their ministry. As you can imagine, this came at a substantial cost, and it resulted in the church incurring debt. When the Great Recession occurred, the corresponding decline in giving and existence of large amounts of debt literally choked out the church's ability to move forward with the ministry vision. In frustration and despondence, Pastor Mike reviewed the past decisions that created the current situation. He analyzed the present and summarized the challenge quite succinctly: "Just as in the story of David and Goliath, we were facing a giant and could not see beyond him."

It was in this process of reviewing the past and analyzing the present that 20/20 clarity arrived. He began to dream of what life would look like if the giant of debt was gone. Pastor Mike and the church leaders started to envision all of the ministry efforts that could be launched if the huge mortgage payment being sent to the bank each month was liberated.

Suddenly, they could see it! The desirable Fully Funded future was in plain sight. When describing the revelation, Pastor Mike shared, "Focus not on the obstacle in front of us, but focus on what's beyond it." It set fire to their focus, energy, and passion. Just a few years later, the church made its final payment on $6.8 million in debt and freed up over $35,000 per month for community impact. He summarized the journey this way, "When fear reigns, we stand still. When faith reigns, we move forward."

NorthStar Church and its members are now living in what was only a dream a few years ago because they chose to embrace the process of clarifying the vision. 20/20 vision gave them all the energy and excitement necessary to embrace the hard work and sacrifice required to accomplish it. The same will happen for you when you seek clarity for your Fully Funded Life.

Ultimately, be certain you understand this fact: there are *future* implications of your *right now* choices. What you determine to do today can have a profound impact on the way you will get to live your life later. Embrace all the frustration of fighting for your Fully Funded Life because, after all, you are worth it!

So far, we have been establishing a foundation for understanding the importance of having 20/20 vision for a Fully Funded Life. We have reviewed the consequences of unclear vision and created guidelines for gaining clarity for your future. Now, the time has finally come to clarify *your* Fully Funded Life.

You can do this!

5

CLARIFYING YOUR FULLY FUNDED LIFE IN 22 QUESTIONS

You are about to embark upon some serious reflection to define what a Fully Funded Life looks like for you. With each question, I encourage you to spend some time in the 20/20 Money Journal writing down your thoughts and ideas. We'll use these later to formulate a financial plan to fund each one.

> Download the Dreams List and other free resources at:
> www.iwbnin.com/2020money

Each question will require different amounts of time and thought. For some people, a question might have a simple and straightforward reply. For others, that same question might require some careful thinking and an extraordinary amount of time. When you encounter one that really challenges you, don't grow weary of the question or skip it. After all, we're talking about *your* Fully Funded Life. It is worth the time and energy required.

Question #1 *What does a Fully Funded Life look like for you?*

Let's focus on the big picture. Before moving on to all of the additional questions, it is important to think about the overall vision you have for your Fully Funded Life. Another way to express this question is: "What does an *abundant life* look like for you?" While you can include some specific details, the key objective is to clarify the overarching dream you have for your life.

For example, I have defined my Fully Funded Life as "being able to help others accomplish far more than they ever thought possible." This is when I feel most alive and fulfilled. I love seeing people experience the "light-bulb moment" that moves them from feeling stuck and sinking to making tremendous progress toward a dream they previously thought was impossible. This applies to my children, my bride, and all those I have the privilege of serving along the way.

If you lack clarity on how to respond to this question, I encourage you to revisit the previous chapter and go through the Romans 12:1-2 process for determining God's will for your life — his good, pleasing, and perfect will. It will help ensure you focus your life on what matters most.

Question #2 *What does "prospering" look like for you?*

I recognize the enormity of this question. It is easy to quickly define prospering as having $1 billion in the bank. However, the real value of this question is to truly define what prospering looks like for *you*, not for Bill Gates, Warren Buffett, Tom Hanks, or LeBron James.

There are people who live in a small home on a country lane who have little financial wealth, but they have zero debt, grow their own food and live off of the land, and raise their children in the great outdoors — and they call it prospering for them. There are many people who don't like the idea of living that way at all! Perhaps their dream is to live in a beachfront condo on the white sand beaches of Destin, Florida, and never have to mow a lawn again in their lifetime. Still others desire to live in Minnesota in the summer and spend their winter months soaking in the sun in the beautiful deserts of Arizona. The answer to this question is different for every single human being. Write down your thoughts as to what true prosperity looks like for you and your family.

Question #3 *Where would you like to travel? When would you like to go there?*

In spite of the efforts of a few "Flat Earthers" to convince us otherwise, the earth is actually round (or mostly round). I am taking this as a sign from God that we should go around it. Where are the places you would like to travel? Think about locations both within the country and also abroad.

This is a good time to issue a public service announcement: don't shut down the dreaming just because you may not have the money for it right now. Write down the dream anyway. Planes, trains, ships, and other vehicles depart daily for nearly every destination. You should be on one of those vehicles arriving at your dream location one day.

I remember the day I wrote down "Visit Hawaii" as one of my travel dreams. At first, it seemed absolutely impossible. Then Jenn and I started to see the finish line of paying off our house, so we planned to take our family to Hawaii to celebrate the accomplishment of eliminating our home mortgage. We paid off our house and, just 13 days later, found out a miracle blessing of a baby girl was headed our way. We were pregnant!

Our Hawaii travel dream was placed on the back burner again as we used the money to pay the insurance deductible. However, just a couple of years later, I was invited to speak in Honolulu. It went so well that we have now been blessed to travel to Hawaii four times. Our dream was everything we thought it would be and more.

I'm so glad we kept the dream alive and refused to give up on it. I encourage you to do the same. Write down all of the places you want to travel. For fun, I encourage you to search the Internet for great travel destinations just to expand your dreaming. If you are going to dream, why not dream big?

Question #4 *What events would you like to attend or participate in?*

Do you want to attend Tulip Time in Pella, Iowa? It's great, and I highly recommend the stroopwafels and poffertjes. Perhaps you would like to go to the Jockey Lot, the Southeast's Biggest and Best Flea Market, located in Anderson, South Carolina, the same town as the world headquarters of I Was Broke. Now I'm Not. If this is one of your dreams, be sure to go on a Saturday or Sunday and get the boiled peanuts. Maybe you would like to attend The Open Championship in the United Kingdom, one of the four annual major golf tournaments, or you might want to see your favorite band play in Tokyo, Japan.

There could be a major annual music festival you would like to attend. The Ark Encounter in Williamstown, Kentucky, is a phenomenal work of craftsmanship that my family really enjoyed. Maybe you are a fan of Laura Ingalls Wilder and the Little House on the Prairie books. You could go see Pa Ingalls' actual fiddle in Mansfield, Missouri.

Are you a runner? Be sure to write down the road races you would like to participate in. I've enjoyed destination races because they help hold me accountable to the preparation required to do well. My first full marathon (26.2 miles!) was at the Rock-N-Roll Marathon hosted in San Diego, California. What a great moment it was to travel across the country and race in the best physical condition I've ever been in!

Seeing a play on Broadway in New York City is a dream for many. For musical and vocal artists, performing at Carnegie Hall is a pinnacle achievement. The Winter and Summer Olympics are amazing gatherings of the world's best athletes, and these contests are hosted every two years. For deep sea fishermen, participating in the White Marlin Open in Ocean City, Florida, is an event they would love to join.

Maybe you want to participate in Oktoberfest in Munich, Germany, or run in the mountains of Salzburg, Austria, just like Julie Andrews in *The Sound of Music*. There is tremendous kayaking to be found in South America. Perhaps you would like to walk the vineyards of France and then go to Venice, Italy, and enjoy a gondola ride. Maybe you would like to chase the Tour de France one summer.

The events we can participate in are wide-ranging and diverse. Be sure to write down all of the ones that interest to you.

Question #5 *Where would you like to live? List the place(s).*

This seemingly simple question really possesses several layers. Is there a specific address or do you have a general area that would be acceptable to you? Some people have a dream to live in the exact house they grew up in, or they desire to live where their grandparents lived. For others, it is more regional. Still others have a desire to live in different locations based on seasons of the year or stages of life.

Many of my friends in the lakes regions have a desire to own a cabin and spend their summers or summer weekends at the lake.

The family cabin becomes a special place for them to make memories that will last a lifetime.

While some have a permanent housing situation in mind— an "until we die" location—others may be more inclined to have dreams that shift as they age and move on to new phases of life. I've seen many people downsize their home in their later years to a place that is easier to maintain. Retirement communities have become a very attractive option for those who are enjoying their golden years.

Do you want to live in the country or the city? Do you want to own acreage or live on a postage stamp lot? Do you want neighbors or not? Do you want to mow grass and maintain a yard? It might be your dream to live in another country entirely! Whatever your dream is, write it down with as much detail as you can.

Question #6 *What type of housing accommodations would you like to live in?*

What type of abode do you desire to dwell in? Many people want to live in a condominium. Others want to live in a ranch house out in the country. Still others don't want a permanent home at all, preferring to own a recreational vehicle and travel the world. You might want to own a mansion complete with a full gymnasium, a garden like those found in European estates, and an infinity pool. Others might want the complete opposite, preferring to have a tiny house.

This may seem like a frivolous exercise to some, but there is tremendous value in considering what your future could look like. Your home is the environment where you will spend the majority of your time, so it will greatly affect the way you live your life. Plus, housing is generally the single largest purchase a person will make in his or her lifetime. It is worth your time to dream about it for a little while.

Question #7 *What are some accomplishments you want to achieve?*

This is where you can ponder specific achievements. What are your educational goals? Is there a particular degree or certification you would like to achieve? Maybe you want to be accepted into a specific school or membership group.

One of my desired goals was to write a book and sell at least one copy to someone other than my mother. I'm grateful to say that goal has been accomplished. Now, it's my desire to have a book sell more than 100,000 copies. The goal after that one? Sell more than 1,000,000 copies. The copy you're holding in your hand has helped move us one copy closer to the goal.

What are some key accomplishments you want to achieve during your lifetime? Do you hope to start and finish a running event—a 5K, a 10K, a half-marathon (13.1 miles), or a full-marathon (26.2 miles)? Maybe you want to complete a full Ironman where you swim 2.4 miles, bike 112 miles, and run 26.2 miles. Maybe your dream is the exact opposite, and you want to live your entire life *without* participating in a road race or Ironman event!

Maybe you want to become a leader of a local organization. Some dream of running for a local political office. Others want to run for a state or provincial-level government office. Still others are aiming to become president or prime minister of their entire country.

Be sure to write down all of the accomplishments you hope to achieve during your lifetime.

Question #8 *Do you want to help your children or grandchildren with educational expenses (private school, college, or training)? If you do, provide details on how you would like to specifically help.*

Is it your desire to help your children achieve certain educational milestones? There are many people who are passionate about homeschooling. Others are excited about providing private school for their children. Education is not cheap. Many families and students are feeling the burden of the extraordinary cost, and it has set them back financially. Do you desire to prevent this from happening to your children or grandchildren?

My twin brother and I were the first in our family to attend and graduate from college. My twin chose to serve in the military which allowed him to graduate without incurring any debt for his undergraduate degree. I chose to date Sallie Mae Student Loan Servicing. This debt followed me around for 8.5 years after I graduated. Many of my college friends are still repaying their student loans more than twenty years after graduation.

My own financial challenges of paying for college compelled me to do whatever it takes to help my own children attend college without debt, so I began saving for their education when my firstborn was four years old. As I am writing this book, she is in the middle of her college studies and on track to graduate free from college debt. It all started with a dream and 20/20 vision on how to fund it.

This is why I am so passionate about helping you really explore all of your plans, hopes, and dreams and clarify your Fully Funded Life. If you know your dreams with 20/20 clarity, you will have a much greater chance of sticking to the decisions, financial and otherwise, necessary to achieve them.

Question #9 *Do you want to start or purchase a business? Detail the type of business you would like to have.*

Many people have an entrepreneurial streak in them and want to start a business. Others would like to buy an existing business. As I outlined in my investing book, *OXEN: The Key to an Abundant Harvest*, birthing a baby business has its challenges, but it can actually be the key source of financial resources, allowing you to fund the wildest dreams of your life. I've found this to be true in my own life as I've birthed four businesses and purchased three others.

Do you want to start a restaurant? If so, what type of food will you serve? What type of environment do you want to create? Maybe it's your dream to purchase an existing plumbing business with the reputation of providing great service for years or even decades.

There are a lot of people who love their favorite fast food restaurant. Why not become a franchise owner and profit from your passion? You might have a hobby you would like to convert into a business. This can be especially rewarding when your hobby actually stops costing you precious money and begins producing it instead.

If you have a business dream, spend some time detailing key aspects you would like it to have: location, timing, and type of product or service you hope to deliver.

Question #10 *Do you want to give money away to help a church, charity, or other worthwhile cause? If so, what specific ones would you like to help?*

Are you passionate about a specific cause or initiative? You can choose to be intentionally generous. If you were winning big-time with your money, what are the additional causes you would want to generously support?

My family is passionate about funding the vision of our local church. Because of this, we bring a tithe of all our gross income to help fund those efforts. We believe the promise from the Lord delivered by the prophet Malachi whose writings are found in the last book of the Old Testament. Malachi 3:10-12 reads:

"10 Bring the whole tithe into the storehouse, that there may be food in my house. Test me in this," says the Lord Almighty, "and see if I will not throw open the floodgates of heaven and pour out so much blessing that there will not be room enough to store it. 11 I will prevent pests from devouring your crops, and the vines in your fields will not drop their fruit before it is ripe," says the Lord Almighty. 12 "Then all the nations will call you blessed, for yours will be a delightful land," says the Lord Almighty."

While I was attending Purdue University, I and my fellow engineering classmates were tasked with writing computer programs. One of the types of commands was an "if-then" statement. It was written to direct the computer to make a decision based upon whether a certain set of conditions were true or not. If a specific condition was met, then the computer was commanded to perform a certain task. If the criteria wasn't met, then the task would be ignored. I guess it can't be helped that I read Malachi's prophecy as an "if-then" statement.

If you bring the whole tithe into the storehouse and *if* you test me in this... *Then* I will open the floodgates of heaven and pour out so much blessing that there will not be room enough to store it. *Then* I will prevent pests from devouring your crops, and the vines in your fields will not drop their fruit before it is ripe. *Then* all the nations will call you blessed, for yours will be a delightful land.

Since Jenn and I both graduated from Purdue University, we donate to this wonderful institution that helped equip us for tremendous success in business and life. We also want to help people we meet along the way who are facing a financial need. This is why we include a line item in our budget each month called "intentionally bless others" where we set aside an amount of money to give away as needs arise.

Bill and Melinda Gates are passionate about improving healthcare globally and reducing extreme poverty.[vi] They have donated a substantial portion of their wealth, billions of dollars, to help fund the causes they are passionate about.

You may not have the wealth of the Gates Family, but you are still able to do something wonderful to help others. Being intentional about your philanthropic efforts is a noble and worthwhile goal, so who and what will you help?

Question #11 *Do you want to position yourself to leave behind an inheritance?*

Proverbs 13:22 shares "A good person leaves an inheritance for their children's children..." In his series, "Positioning Yourself to Prosper," Bishop T. D. Jakes exclaimed, "One of the curses that is killing our generation... [is] because most of us start from ground-level-zero. We start out with nothing. All over again. Your parents started with nothing. They died and left you nothing. You go back to zero and have to start over again. That is a curse! The curse of not having anything left." He then connected this thought directly to leaving an inheritance when he said, "Consequently, because nobody gave to you, you don't think generationally."[vii]

Are you thinking generationally and considering the legacy you will leave behind?

Of course, an inheritance can be about so much more than money. You can focus on intentionally leaving an inheritance of faith, possessions, knowledge, and love. One of the greatest things we can leave our children and children's children is wonderful memories of experiences shared together!

One day I had the joy of visiting the local branch of my bank in Anderson, South Carolina. I showed up at a busy time and had the pleasure of waiting in line along with around ten other people. One of the ladies waiting in line with us was at least 80 years old. She was dressed up and ready to mingle! I don't know her name, so I'm going to call her Bank Lady. Well, Bank Lady was soon tired of waiting, and she got out of line and started talking to anyone who would listen — and several who wouldn't. You did not need to eavesdrop on her conversations because she was talking very loudly.

As she progressed back through the line of people, Bank Lady stopped short at another lady in line who was wearing traditional African attire. For clarity in this story, let's call her Nice Lady.

"You ain't from around here, are you?" Bank Lady asked loudly.

"No, ma'am, I'm not," replied Nice Lady with a distinct accent.

"Where are you from?" Bank Lady asked.

"I am from Kenya," Nice Lady responded.

Bank Lady broke into a huge smile and shouted loudly, "Well … Ken-ya (can ya) help me? This line is moving too slow!"

The entire line of people was now listening intently waiting to see where Bank Lady was going with this conversation and how Nice Lady was going to respond.

Before Nice Lady could attempt a response, Bank Lady continued, "I've been there! No, seriously! I've been there!" Bank Lady then shared an amazing story of how her father arranged a trip around the world for their family when she was a young teenager. She shared how they sailed out of New York Harbor in the spring and went on a months-long trip around the world. She described how, during the trip, she visited Kenya and shared how much the country had impressed her. She talked about the beauty of the people and the country's natural wonders.

The conversation was a wonderful distraction from the normal frustration of waiting in line at the bank. In fact, everyone in line enjoyed the story.

As I left the bank, I was marked by their conversation. Here's why. I saw Bank Lady, an elderly woman still full of life, sharing how her daddy had given her an amazing gift she could carry all of the days of her life. It was a gift of a memorable shared experience. The lasting present of a wonderful shared experience. Her parents had given her an inheritance beyond just money!

Even though this happened several years ago, I can still see Bank Lady's eyes shining and her broad smile as she described her trip and how she connected with Nice Lady deeply during a simple visit to the local bank. Remember: a dream sets the eyes agleam!

It was then that I made a decision to not only leave a financial inheritance but to leave an inheritance of memories and shared experiences. I want my children's eyes to shine when, at the age of eighty, they describe the experiences they shared alongside mom and dad with people waiting in line at the bank.

I suspect you probably have shared similar wonderful experiences with your parents and grandparents. When people have lost their precious loved one, it can be natural to move from rejoicing in the happy memories to feeling overwhelmed by grief. If this is the case for you, let me share a quote from Dr. Seuss that has been helpful to me. Dr. Seuss said, "Don't cry because it's over. Smile because it happened."

Bank Lady smiled because it happened. Her very soul smiled that day.

Many people desire to give some inheritance money away to charitable causes as one of their last acts on this earth. This can even be set up in a way that allows a person to give wealth away while living and produce income until their death. This is accomplished through charitable trusts and gift annuities.

Many people have chosen to give away some of the inheritance to their heirs while still alive, choosing to assist with education, vacations, cars, and the like. This allows them to see, feel, and experience the joy such gifts can provide their heirs.

What is your goal for the wealth and possessions you will leave behind? Be sure to think beyond just the dollars and consider family heirlooms and other things that are important for you to pass on to the next generation.

Question #12 *Would you like to go on missions trips? What specific type of missions would you like to participate in?*

Missions can be as simple as serving in a local food pantry for a few hours to choosing to move and live for years in a community far away from your home. Many churches organize local, regional, national, and international missions trips.

One doesn't have to travel too far from home to see unmet needs. Many fantastic organizations have been developed to connect willing and able people with those who are less fortunate. If this is something you are particularly passionate about, be sure to include missions as part of your plans, hopes, and dreams.

Question #13 *Is it your dream to retire? If so, write down your thoughts as to when you would like to retire and what retirement looks like for you in your Fully Funded Life.*

The idea of retirement is overwhelming for many people. Many people struggle to move from being a wage-earner to relying on their investments to carry the financial load. It is challenging for many to cease their daily work all at once, so they merge into retirement, choosing to scale back over a period of time.

Are you planning to retire in five years or fifty? Some people target a specific age in which they plan to retire. Many times, this is directly connected to a pension plan requiring a specific age or years of service or a combination of both. Maybe your retirement is dependent upon achieving a certain amount of money in your investment accounts, a set number of rental homes, when grandchildren show up on the scene, or some other metric.

What do you plan to do with your time once you retire? Many people plan to travel a lot. Others decide to stay at home and volunteer. Be sure to give this considerable thought as it is essential in preparing for the big day when you actually retire.

Stewart Friedman is the Practice Professor Emeritus of Management and Director of the Wharton Work/Life Integration Project. He has focused his work on understanding the balance of work and life. Regarding retirement, he shares, "The most successful people in retirement look to use their talents and passions to make a contribution."[viii] He adds, "It's critical to reflect on what matters to you. People at this stage are focused on their legacy. You need to actively inquire of yourself: What do I want to leave behind?" These are great thoughts to consider as you approach retirement planning.

Question #14 *Do you desire to have a second home — a beach house, mountain cabin, lake house, or something else? Write your dream down!*

Is it your dream to have a second home? A second home can actually serve more than one purpose. It can not only fulfill a dream, but it can also generate income, increase retirement savings, and provide years of memories for your family.

One of my friends always dreamed of owning a beach home. During the great recession, he purchased a home for nearly half the price it was valued at just a couple of years prior. It had a vacation rental history of many years showing that families would rent the home for the exact same week each year for their summer vacation. It had positive cash flow from the very first day of ownership. More than a decade later, the property has doubled in value and rents have skyrocketed. He is really happy he chose to chase his beach house dream. Make sure you do the same. It starts with spending some time thinking about whether or not a second home is part of your future Fully Funded Life.

Question #15 *Do you have a specific vehicle (or vehicles) you would like to own? Car, truck, boat, side-by-side, snow machine, tractor, etc.*

Many people have emotional connections to their vehicles. For many, it is a specific vehicle. Maybe it is a Chevy Corvette. Perhaps it is a 1967 Ford Mustang Shelby GT500. Some people enjoy creating their own custom vehicles. Write down the ones you would enjoy owning for a while.

If you have heard me speak, you have probably heard about my passion for tractors—especially the green kind. I enjoy climbing up on the John Deere tractor and putting some time in the fields literally living out the principle of sowing and reaping. Whatever your dream vehicles, machines, and equipment are, be sure to write them down.

A Broader Perspective

Now, it is time to spend time thinking about bigger picture items that are vitally important to fully defining your Fully Funded Life. For many people, these questions are more challenging because they are harder to quantify, but these are the very areas of life that can greatly hinder your ability to live the way you desire. I encourage you to spend quality time considering and responding to each question.

Question #16 *What do you believe you need to live free of financial stress?*

When I teach in live events, I always ask people to write down some of their plans, hopes, and dreams. Without fail, "reducing financial stress" is the number one reason people want to win with money. It is clear; money causes a lot of people an extraordinary amount of pain and suffering, so let's think about what life would look like without the stress.

What would allow you to live free of financial stress?

Let me share what helped out my family in a huge way: paying off all of our non-house debt. When we eliminated our car payment, truck payment, credit card debt, and student loans, it freed up more than just money in our monthly budget. It relieved financial stress. We were able to utilize the newly liberated monthly payments to build up our savings accounts, increase our investments, and begin to fund our plans, hopes, and dreams. It sped up our climb toward a Fully Funded Life.

One other major contributing factor to financial stress in marriages is a "non-participating spouse." When one spouse chooses not to participate in dreaming about the future and refuses to make the financial decisions necessary to achieve a Fully Funded Life, it can lead to a lot of friction. If you are facing this situation, take heart. I used to be a non-participating spouse! Now, not only have I become fully engaged in dreaming about the future and making good financial decisions, but I also teach, speak, and write about money. A turnaround is possible.

What does living free of financial stress look like for you and your family? Is it the achievement of total debt freedom— including your home? Is it a certain amount of monthly income?

Perhaps it is a specific amount put away in your saving and investment accounts. Take some time to ponder how you can reduce or eliminate financial stress in your life.

Question #17 *What are your relationship goals?*

Some people want to get married and have kids and grandkids. Others desire to remain single. Few things have the ability to affect your entire life — financially and otherwise — like your relationships. We are the sum of our relationships. The people you associate with have a profound and direct impact on your ability to achieve your Fully Funded Life.

This is intensified when considering a marriage relationship. As the old saying goes, marriage is grand and divorce, well, that's at least one hundred grand. Knowing this, it is wildly important to set goals. For me, one of my goals is to be married to Jenn Sangl for all of her life. Of course, it must work both ways, so it is also my goal for it to be Jenn Sangl's goal to be married to me for all of my life!

Review your friendships, colleagues, and family and set some goals. If you have any toxic relationships, consider how you might need to redefine them so they do not adversely affect your ability to achieve a Fully Funded Life.

Question #18 *For those with children or planning to have them, what are your dreams? Do you desire to be a stay-at-home parent? List the goals you have for your children or grandchildren.*

Children are indeed a blessing from the Lord, but they are really expensive. What are the dreams you have for your children? Think about the values you want to instill in them. College expenses continue to increase. Is it your desire to help your children or grandchildren graduate from college without any student loan debt?

I graduated from college with a lot of student loan debt. After feeling the pain of repaying these loans for several years, it was clear this was something I wanted to help my children avoid. Thankfully for my family, our financial wakeup call happened when our firstborn daughter arrived on the scene. Because we had written down our dream to help our children with college, it motivated us to open a 529 college savings plan and establish automatic monthly contributions. Imagine the satisfaction we felt as we walked onto various college campuses in our daughter's college search knowing her college education was fully funded. It was all made possible because we chose to write down the dream as part of our Fully Funded Life.

The same will be true for you when you begin to write down the dreams. Think about it. Is there really anything greater than being able to bless your children and grandchildren? Write down all the big dreams you have for them.

Question #19 *What are your health goals? Lifestyle, fitness level, nutrition, etc.*

"Fill your brain with knowledge, but always remember this: Your body carries your brain." I heard this statement long ago, and it really connected with me. If I don't take care of my body, it could fail prematurely. It won't matter what I've done to gain knowledge. Of course, no one is going to live forever, but it is important to have a vision for how you would like to live during your one and only life.

I love the outdoors. It is my passion to spend as much time outside as possible. I enjoy gardening, hunting, fishing, running, playing sports, swimming, boating, hiking, and exploring. This requires a tremendous level of fitness. This is why I always set an annual running goal. As I write this book, I am actively working on my goal to run 450 miles this year. Every time I complete a run, an app on my phone updates me with the total miles I have run and provides a chart showing my progress versus my goal. The accountability is very helpful. It also tells me where each run ranks versus all of the others I have completed. My last run was my 426th fastest. On second thought, I'm not sure how I feel about this sort of accountability!

When you look at the dreams that comprise a Fully Funded Life for you, what level of health and fitness will be required? Be sure to add these goals to your list.

Question #20 *What are your spiritual goals?*

Do you have any specific spiritual goals that would help you live your Fully Funded Life? Some goals can include reading the entire Bible, consistent prayer and fasting, church membership and attendance, discipleship, outreach, missions, and personal evangelism.

Another great goal to consider is pursuing contentment and generosity. Your stewardship practices have a profound effect on your ability to grow spiritually.

Numerous studies have demonstrated that spiritually active people live longer. In one study, it showed that women who attended church more than once a week had a 33% less chance of dying during the study's 16-year study-follow-up period.[ix]

As with any other goal, personal discipline is vitally important to achieving your desired spiritual growth. Write down all of the ways you want to grow spiritually.

Question #21 *What are your career goals? Think about position, influence, and impact.*

For many people, career goals dictate much of their lives. It sets their daily schedule, determines where they live, who they associate with, and establishes their economic position. What are your career goals? Perhaps you desire to work the same job for 40 years and retire. Others plan to work a particular position for 18 months and move up the ladder as they chase their aspirations to lead a Fortune 500 company.

Since your job can have such a profound impact on the rest of your life, it certainly makes sense to spend a considerable amount of time spent thinking about your various career goals — including position, influence, impact, income, locations, and experiences.

Question #22 *Are there any specific things you absolutely despise dealing with and want to avoid if at all possible?*

When I was a kid, one of the biggest highlights was being able to spend the day at the huge theme park, riding roller coasters, seeing the variety of shows, and visiting the water park. The closest one to my house was Kings Island, just outside of Cincinnati, Ohio. My mother had to keep track of six rowdy sons, and I'm sure it wasn't always the most enjoyable experience for her. In a recent conversation about visiting theme parks, Mom announced that she has placed visiting such places on her "reverse bucket list."

I had heard of "bucket lists" before—all of those things a person wants to accomplish or experience in his or her lifetime. This "reverse bucket list" was a new concept for me. Her explanation of this new terminology was quite simple: "Things on my reverse bucket list are things I'm never going to do again."

This is an important thing to consider when defining your Fully Funded Life! What are the things you absolutely never want to do again, if at all possible to avoid, in the future?

Jenn and I have watched our fair share of home renovation television shows. When I left corporate America to pursue my dream of teaching personal finances full-time, it seemed to be an appropriate time for us to buy a "fixer upper" and try our hand at building sweat equity. After all, the people hosting every show we watched were able to flip the house in about sixty minutes, and they almost always made a ton of money. I'm sure you know where our story is going. The entire process was an unmitigated disaster—financially, relationally, and architecturally. Suffice it to say that we have put "personal home renovations" on our reverse bucket list. We will be very happy living our Fully Funded Lives free of fixer uppers.

Of course, you can't avoid all painful or frustrating circumstances in life, but you can prevent many of them by writing them down as part of what your Fully Funded Life will *not* include.

Final Question *On a scale of 1 (not even close) to 10 (beyond wildest dreams), where are you now compared to where you dreamed you would be by this age/stage of life?*

Not even close		Running Behind		On Track		Ahead of schedule		Beyond wildest dreams	
1	2	3	4	5	6	7	8	9	10

It is important to be honest with yourself as this is a huge question that helps define your Fully Funded Life.

Before moving on, consider the wording I used in the last sentence. There is a key word in it: Honest. This is all about you and your Fully Funded Life. If you fail to be completely truthful in answering and responding to all of these questions, who will it hurt? You!

This isn't about comparing yourself to other people. None of this is about how much others have accomplished. It is all about your wiring, your calling, your desires, your make-up, your passions, and your life. It is solely and exclusively about you. You are uniquely and wonderfully made. You are one-of-a-kind. No one has the same fingerprint as you. In facial recognition software, there isn't another person on the planet who will match you.

You are *worth* spending time on. As you move through all of these questions with a clear and truthful mindset, you will probably encounter the comparison game. Your mind will want to wander to what others want you to do, how they want you to behave, and what they have accomplished in their own lives. Don't let it happen! As we established in the chapter focused on setting guidelines for defining your Fully Funded Life, when you offer yourself as a living sacrifice and are transformed by the renewing of your mind, you will be able to know your calling—yours alone.

Do you see how important it is that you answer this question honestly? If you do, perhaps it is appropriate to ask the question one more time just to be certain you've been fully truthful with yourself.

Final Question *On a scale of 1 (not even close) to 10 (beyond wildest dreams), where are you now compared to where you dreamed you would be by this age/stage of life?*

Not even close		Running Behind		On Track		Ahead of schedule		Beyond wildest dreams	
1	2	3	4	5	6	7	8	9	10

Is your answer the same or did you need to modify it? If it is the same, wonderful. If you changed it, think about what lie you were believing that made you provide a less than honest answer the first time around. Don't be ashamed of it because this process of truthful self-evaluation is essential to fully knowing yourself. Self-awareness will help pave the path to build tremendous confidence in who you are and where you are headed with your Fully Funded Life.

Before moving on …

Now that you've seen all of the questions, can I ask you to do something? It is really an important request. Will you stop right here in this book and take some time to dream? Will you please go through each of these questions and answer them for your own life?

The remainder of this book is focused on helping you fund your Fully Funded Life. If you haven't taken time to write your dreams down, the guidance provided will seem more applicable to someone other than you. However, when you have written down your plans, hopes, and dreams, it is going to generate special energy and passion that will help you employ the financial steps necessary to fund your future. Most of us require this special energy to power through the tough financial decisions necessary to live a Fully Funded Life.

WAIT!

Did you take time to clearly outline what your Fully Funded Life looks like?

If you did not take the time to clearly outline your Fully Funded Life, please go back through each question and document your thoughts! My direction to you is similar to the game of Monopoly®. While you don't have to go directly to jail, the rest of the instructions apply: Do not pass go. Do not collect $200. Go directly back to the start of this chapter, and answer all of the questions.

Once you have documented all of your God-given plans, hopes, and dreams, proceed to the next chapter where you will begin to learn how to fund each one of them.

6

CONNECTING THE VISION TO YOUR MONEY

When my firstborn daughter, Melea, was about four years old, we visited a neighbor's yard sale. Immediately, Melea spied a dirt bike and decided to implement her negotiating skills.

"I want to buy your motorcycle. I'll give you a dollar for it," Melea said to our neighbor. It was so cute that the neighbor couldn't bring himself to deliver the sad news directly, so he responded with a smile, "I'm sorry, but the motorcycle costs a little more than that."

My daughter immediately caved in on her negotiating approach and went all-in with her highest and best offer: "Okay, I'll give you two dollars." I can still hear the "I can't really believe I'm offering you this much, but…" tone in which she delivered her counteroffer.

She didn't close the deal.

Through this failed negotiation, I saw Melea begin to understand a very important life lesson: dreams come with a cost. This is an important fact to understand when dreaming of your Fully Funded Life. Everything you are dreaming of accomplishing will have a financial cost.

My daughter was able to easily dream of owning a motorcycle, but her financial position at the age of four prevented the dream from becoming a reality. She had no problem dreaming, but she had a funding issue. As adults, we tend to have the opposite issue. Our ability to dream has been stunted because we immediately think of the financial reality. We know the cost. In addition, we know how much we need to work to produce that amount of money. Just thinking of the cost and work required is enough to drain away most, if not all, of our enthusiasm for the dream.

Thus far, I have been encouraging you to dream without considering the financial implications or cost. Now, it is time to understand the full price of your dreams and formulate a plan of action to achieve them. Of course, this is where many people become very discouraged and want to give up on dreaming altogether. Don't let this be the case for you. Achieving your dreams makes it necessary to learn how to navigate tough decisions.

It is time to categorize your dreams based on when you would like to achieve each one. Place each dream into the appropriate time period.

- In the next 12 months
- 1 to 5 years from now
- 6 to 10 years from now
- 11 to 20 years from now
- 21+ years from now

Download the Dreams List and other free resources at:
www.iwbnin.com/2020money

It is important to consider the time period for when you would like to achieve each dream because it has a profound effect on the options available for funding it. The longer term your dream, the more you can take advantage of investing and the power of compound interest. Your shorter-term dreams will require more innovative approaches. Investing and innovative approaches are tremendously interesting to me. How about you?

Identify the Types of Costs for Each Dream.

As we connect your plans, hopes, and dreams to your money, it is important to start thinking through the financial implications of each goal. How much does each one really cost and what type of costs are associated with it? When considering the types of costs, categorize them into two buckets: one-time cost and ongoing cost. I call the dreams with one-time costs, "Moment Dreams" and the ones with ongoing costs, "Lifestyle Dreams." Let's review each type.

Moment Dreams (One-time Cost)

Many dreams have a single, one-time cost. This includes goals like going on a vacation or attending a concert performance by your favorite band. There is a cost, but the expenses cease once the trip or event is over. These can be more straight-forward to plan for financially.

For one particular spring break, I decided it was time for our family to go to Disney World. While it came at a cost, the vacation had a set price. It was expensive, yet magical, and it provided many wonderful memories our family will share forever. Thankfully, there were no additional ongoing costs for us to cover once we left the park.

Common Moment Dreams include:

1. Vacations
2. Home projects (kitchen renovation, landscaping, window replacement, maintenance project, new roof, etc.)
3. Events (concerts, sporting events, festivals, etc.)
4. Furniture
5. Charitable gifts (church building project, helping another person, supporting a worthwhile cause)

Other dreams come with an upfront cost that is just the beginning of your financial journey with them. I call them Lifestyle Dreams.

Lifestyle Dreams (Upfront Cost plus Ongoing Costs)

For Lifestyle Dreams, it is imperative to understand the ongoing costs required to sustain or maintain them. Acquiring a Lifestyle goal is just the beginning of the financial journey with it. A common Lifestyle dream is home ownership. I'll never forget the day Jenn and I bought our first home in 1998. We paid $115,900. After the closing, I went back to my workplace feeling quite elated about our big purchase. Doug Smith, a fellow engineer who was about 15 years older than me, said, "Congratulations! You are now owned by a home."

At first, I was confused by his apparent misstatement. I quickly realized it was an intentional bending of the phrase. Anyone who has ever owned a home before knows Doug was absolutely correct.

There were a lot of ongoing costs related to this purchase, financial and otherwise. Apparently, we needed furniture. I was content to sleep on the floors, but my bride thought otherwise. We also needed curtains. The grass grew, and I found myself at the store purchasing a lawn mower. Then I discovered there was an ongoing time cost because I found myself pushing the mower around the yard on a weekly basis. Of course, we had additional ongoing costs such as home insurance, annual property taxes, and PMI. Living in South Carolina, we discovered it was wildly important to pay the monthly price of electricity so we could have air conditioning and lights. We heated the house with natural gas which came with an additional monthly toll. We chose to sign up for Internet and cable television which incurred another monthly fee. Home ownership is clearly a Lifestyle dream!

Here are some common Lifestyle dreams:

- Real Estate (cost to purchase plus ongoing taxes, insurance, utilities, HOA fees, and maintenance)
- Automobiles, Boats, and Motorcycles (acquisition cost plus ongoing taxes, insurance, and maintenance)
- Cell phone (purchase price plus ongoing service provider contract fees)
- Small Business (start-up costs plus ongoing operating expenses, overhead, payroll, taxes, and licenses)
- Ongoing Charitable Giving (tithing and monthly support of a worthwhile cause)

Review your dreams list. What type of costs will it take to achieve each one? Which ones are one-time, Moment Dreams with a single cost? Which ones are Lifestyle Dreams, having an acquisition cost while also requiring an ongoing financial commitment?

Begin your assessment by focusing on dreams in the "within the next 12 months" category. Then move on to the "1 to 5 years from now" dreams. Continue this assessment until you've categorized all of your dreams as "Moment" or "Lifestyle."

Determine the actual costs of each dream.

Once you have categorized each dream, it is important to look at the costs of each one. Again, begin with the "within the next 12 months" list of dreams, and write down your best educated guess of the cost required to achieve or acquire each one. If it is a Lifestyle Dream, make sure you document the various costs required to sustain it.

For your short-term dreams, it is important to clearly understand their actual specific costs. As you begin to consider funding your longer-term dreams, it is more acceptable to provide a rough estimate. If you are struggling to determine the costs of a particular dream, spend a few minutes searching on Google and this should help provide some clarity.

As you consider the costs, do you feel any anxiety? If so, then now is a great time to remind you that these dreams will most likely cost far more than your current income and funding methods can currently support. It is, after all, the nature of dreams to be expensive. You will face challenges to their accomplishment, and money will surely be one of them.

> It is, after all, the nature of dreams to be expensive.

One of the great causes of anxiety is lack of knowledge. This process will help inform and educate you, so try to put aside your doubts, misgivings, fears, and anxiety and spend some time right now researching and documenting the costs of each of your dreams on the Dreams List.

Understand the Opportunity Costs of Each Dream.

There is an economic principle called opportunity cost. It is defined as the benefit that must be given up to achieve or acquire something else. It is important to understand how this may relate to each of your dreams. As you look at your Dreams List, are there any dreams that compete with each other? For example, one person has a dream to raise their kids in a subdivision but also dreams of living on a farm way out in the country at least one mile from another human being. Unless this person finds a subdivision with lots measured in square miles, these two dreams are mutually exclusive. One will have to be relinquished—either to be pursued later in life or abandoned altogether.

> Download the Dreams List and other free resources at:
> www.iwbnin.com/2020money

Other dreams may compete for the exact some funding source. If most of your dreams are being funded by the income created by your job, there's a good chance some of the dreams will have to be moved, delayed, or abandoned. This is the opportunity cost one must pay in order to secure the dreams he or she feels is more important and valuable.

One dream I have is to power my house with solar panels. It is beneficial to the environment and has the potential to completely eliminate my electric bill. This is a Moment Dream that comes with a substantial price tag, even with substantial federal and state rebates. This is yet another time where I must evaluate the opportunity costs. If I use money on this project, I won't be able to keep it in savings. I lose that opportunity. I also will lose the chance to use the money to fund other dreams like vacations and financial gifts I want to give away to worthwhile causes. I also forfeit the opportunity to use it to purchase an investment like real estate or a small business. This is where having extreme clarity provided by 20/20 vision helps me make the decision much more easily.

Once you have categorized each dream and documented the costs associated with each one, it is time to identify ways to fund them. We'll explore this fun and challenging topic next.

7

FUNDING YOUR DREAMS

It is time to figure out how to make each dream become a reality — at least from a financial standpoint. This is the fun part! There are many ways to generate money. Before you decide on how you will fund each of your dreams, it is important to understand how other people have done it. Here are some of the more common methods people have employed to fund dreams.

Income from Regular Job

For most people, their initial funding method will be through their own personal income generated from working a job. As Dave Ramsey has said, "Your most powerful wealth-building tool is your income…"[x] It's true. If you can work a job and produce income, you are able to begin chasing your dreams.

If you have debt right now, consider this thought: what would your finances look like right now if you had zero debt payments? What if you had no car payment, no student loan payment, zero credit card payments, no furniture payment, and no personal loans? What could you do with all of the payments that currently go to service debt each month? You could fund a lot of dreams right away, couldn't you?

Ultimately, this is where many people become very limited in their thinking. This is because, for most people, their income allows them to sustain the basics of life, and they cannot accommodate extra costs. Even if you work half-days—you know the type I am talking about—working true half-days: 12 hours per day, the amount of money you can produce is still limited. To fund big-time dreams, you must find ways to earn money without having to work for all of it. This is why it is so important to free up money from debt. It allows you to use your money to make more money for you.

Income from a Second (or Third) Job

Many people become so highly energized by this process of chasing dreams that they choose to work more. Is it because they are gluttons for work? Probably not! It is because they can *see* their dreams being funded in the future by choosing to sacrifice some extra time and energy right now. They have 20/20 vision. Working additional jobs is an excellent way to fund additional dreams in the short-term. It comes with an added bonus in that the extra time spent working provides less time for spending.

This is exactly how I was able to fund my dream of publishing a book. In addition to my regular job, I had been accepting opportunities to speak at various churches and businesses. I used the extra income generated from these events to grow our savings account. When the time came to publish my first book, *I Was Broke. Now I'm Not.*, we were in the financial position to pay for the printing of 3,000 copies.

Bonus (Quarterly, Semi-annually, Annually, Randomly)

This is something many people receive from their employer. If this is something that occurs at your workplace, you can choose to direct these extra funds toward funding your dreams. It is far more exciting to use a bonus to fund a dream than to use it to catch up on unpaid bills that have resulted from poor financial behavior. Nothing is more disheartening than receiving a bonus and realizing the money is dead on arrival because you have to use it to satisfy a debt created by a bad spending decision.

In my brief career in corporate America, I was lucky enough to receive a few bonuses. In fact, we utilized the last couple of bonuses to accomplish Rung #4 of the I Was Broke. Now I'm Not. Ladder: "Eliminate all non-house, non-business debt." What a wonderful day it was in February 2004 when we were able to achieve our dream of becoming debt-free — except for the home mortgage.

Tax Refunds

The old argument was that receiving a tax refund was like giving the government a no-interest loan. The logic for this argument faded away as interest rates on savings dwindled down to nearly 0% through the Great Recession. In reality, tax refunds can be a sort of forced savings allowing the recipient to receive a large lump sum of money. It can be an excellent way to fund some dreams.

I utilized my tax refund in 2003 to fund my dream of achieving Rung #2 of the I Was Broke. Now I'm Not. Ladder: "Save money — start with one month of expenses." It was a great decision and introduced my family to the tremendous value of having financial margin.

Inheritance

Through the ages, inheritance money has been utilized to help the next generation advance their financial position and fund dreams. Anyone who has received an inheritance knows this money comes attached to some tremendous emotions due to the loss of a beloved person who bequeathed it. I would encourage anyone who receives an inheritance to place the money in savings for at least a year to ensure these emotions do not lead to poor financial decisions.

Consider this thought: If a person has left an inheritance to a loved one, would they desire it to bless their heirs and help them advance toward their dreams or would they rather the heirs waste it in a frivolous and wild manner? I am confident they would want it to be a blessing to each of them. If you receive an inheritance, be sure to honor the giver of the blessing by utilizing it to advance toward your Fully Funded Life.

Stock Investments

This can be an excellent way to fund dreams over the longer term. In general, this type of funding method is appropriate for dreams you would like to fund more than five years from now. This is because of the up-and-down nature of the overall stock market. More than 95% of five-year periods of the stock market have made money. Many companies also share profits, called dividends, with their shareholders which can help hasten the funding of their dreams.

I used this method to fund our family's trip to Disney World. I purchased four company stocks and sold them seven years later at a substantial profit. It funded the entire trip, including our stay at Disney's Boardwalk Inn. Mickey Mouse gladly accepted the money, and our entire family had a magical time building memories we will treasure for a lifetime without incurring any debt.

Mutual Fund Investments

Mutual fund investments provide additional protection against the potential loss of money because they are diversified. While the fund holds stock investments, it isn't just the stocks of one or two companies. The average mutual fund has 200 to 1,000 company stocks, bonds, and other investments. As those investments grow in value and pay dividends and interest, those organizations will help you fund your dreams.

Solomon speaks to the importance of having diversified investments in the book of Ecclesiastes. He wrote in Ecclesiastes 11:2, "Invest in seven ventures, yes, in eight; you do not know what disaster may come upon the land."

You may have heard the common cliché: don't put all of your eggs into one basket. I have experienced the truth of this exact principle. Since achieving our dream of living in the country several years ago, I have had chickens on the farm. Every day, most of my hens will lay an egg. After a couple of days away on a business trip, I came home to discover 18 eggs in the nest boxes. I gathered them all together into my egg basket and headed toward the house. I'm sure you can guess what happened. That's right. I tripped and fell. Every single one of those eggs shattered. Even through my frustration at my clumsiness and loss of so many eggs, I managed to smile because I knew the principle was true!

Because of the diversification provided by mutual funds, tens of millions of people have chosen this method to help fund their retirement dreams.

Real Estate Investments

Through the ages, real estate has been one of the keys to building substantial wealth and funding huge dreams. In fact, real estate is connected not only to wealth in the Bible, but it is also tied to generosity. Acts 4:33b-35 shares "...and God's grace was so powerfully at work in them all [34] that there were no needy persons among them. For from time to time those who owned land or houses sold them, brought the money from the sales [35] and put it at the apostles' feet, and it was distributed to anyone who had need. [36] Joseph, a Levite from Cyprus, whom the apostles called Barnabas (which means "son of encouragement"), [37] sold a field he owned and brought the money and put it at the apostles' feet."

They sold "land or houses" to help others. Joseph sold a field in a generous act. What is another way of saying this? They sold real estate to help others.

While not a perfect fit for everyone, rental houses, commercial property, and raw land have the potential to fund huge dreams in your life. Make sure you consider this as part of your dream funding plan.

Small Business

Small businesses are the heartbeat of any growing economy. Entrepreneurial people see a need and find a way to provide solutions to solve it. As a result, economies and countries move forward. The small business owner can be rewarded along the way with profits dwarfing the amount of money they could have ever earned through a job. The beauty of small business is the ability to utilize the skills sets and energies of other people and technologies. This can result in a multiplying effect for the finances of the small business owner. This, in turn, enables them to fund their biggest dreams.

This is a method I have chosen to help fund my dreams. I began with one business idea and began to develop it. I started I Was Broke. Now I'm Not. to help people win with their money. I wrote a book with that title, and the rest is history. We have been blessed enough to grow to a point where I now own seven small businesses.

Franchise

A franchise is a type of small business that comes with existing sales and marketing systems, financial controls, employee training, and business systems. It allows people to embark on the small business journey without having to create and innovate every single part of it along the way. McDonald's, Taco Bell, Ace Hardware, Fairfield Inn & Suites, Maaco, Stanley Steemer, Sport Clips, and Gold's Gym are all examples of franchises owned by individuals or small business groups. This funding method can have a profound effect on your ability to accomplish the biggest dreams of your life.

If you are intrigued by franchising and want to learn more while also being entertained, spend an evening watching the movie, *The Founder*. It tells the story behind the creation of the McDonald's franchise and can help you understand the value of being part of a franchised company.

Buying and Reselling

Buying and reselling is a time-tested way to produce extra money to fund dreams. Whether you like to buy and resell cars, antiques, hobby equipment, or cosmetic products, there has never been an easier time to match up buyers with sellers. While you can sell in-person, the explosion of options on the Internet have connected buyers around the planet. Craigslist, eBay, and Amazon provide platforms for billions of dollars to exchange hands.

Retirement Account

Whether you are investing in a 401(k), 403(b), 457, IRA, Roth IRA, SEP-IRA, SIMPLE IRA, TFSA, or RRSP, these investment vehicles can be an excellent tax-advantaged way to fund dreams during your retirement years. It can allow you to venture into retirement with confidence that you can travel, enjoy family and friends, and provide for yourself for the rest of your life.

Within these accounts, you have access to several of the funding methods already covered with one great and powerful added benefit: tax advantages!

Retirement Pension

Provided for many employees as part of their overall compensation plan, pension payments can allow a person to enter retirement knowing some, or perhaps all, of their monthly financial needs will be met. This funding vehicle can provide great confidence to a person when considering their longer-term plans, hopes, and dreams.

Social Security Income

As you contribute a portion of every paycheck to the Social Security Trust (FICA: Federal Insurance Contributions Act), you are funding part of your retirement. While it requires mandatory participation, it can provide an excellent additional source of funds to cover basic financial needs. If you follow the I Was Broke. Now I'm Not. Ladder and arrive at Rung #9 by the time you enter retirement, it is quite likely your social security checks will be able to be used exclusively for funding additional dreams.

Annuities

An annuity can allow you to secure a guaranteed payment at a set frequency for the remainder of your life. While it can be an expensive way to eliminate risk, millions of people have made the choice that the cost was worth guaranteeing income for the rest of their lives. If you have an annuity, this money could be a potential funding source for your dreams.

Savings: Savings Accounts, Certificate of Deposit (CD), and Money Market Account

While money placed in a savings account will not grow rapidly, it can provide a modest amount of interest which can be used to fund dreams. Saved money helps a person achieve Rungs #2 and #5 on the I Was Broke. Now I'm Not. Ladder, and this alone could be a personal dream for a family to achieve as it provides a measure of financial freedom and reduces financial stress.

Private Investors and Partnerships

Many dreams will require more money than all of your funding sources could support—even if they were all put together. This is a great time to obtain an investor or business partnership. While the cost of a particular dream might be overwhelming for you and your finances, it might be quite easy for someone else to fund it. Many great dreams have been able to become a reality because of one person's vision and another's money.

Steve Jobs and Steve Wozniak, the founders of Apple Computer started their company with a third partner. You may not have heard of Ronald Wayne before, but as the third partner, he wrote the company's partnership agreement, illustrated the first Apple logo, and wrote the Apple I manual.[xi] The young fledgling company also needed capital investment and found it in their next hire, Mike Markkula. Mike brought in $250,000 of his own money, $80,000 as an equity investment and $170,000 as a loan. With this transaction, Markkula became a one-third owner of Apple Computer, holding an equal share with Jobs and Wozniak.[xii] Even though most people think only of Jobs and Wozniak when looking at Apple's tremendous success, it was through a series of partnerships and private investment like the ones with Wayne and Markkula that the company was able to move forward through the early years.

Crowdfunding

If you have a great business or product idea, consider pitching it to the masses. The advent of the Internet and ongoing improvement in ecommerce has enabled the entire world to learn about and participate in funding good ideas and projects. Websites like Kickstarter and GoFundMe have helped connect people with good ideas to others who possess the ability to fund them. One project, the Pebble Time watch (think about an early version of Apple Watch) used Kickstarter and raised $20,338,986 from 78,471 backers![xiii] This means the average investor put in $259.19 to support the launch of this project. Apparently, the technology was good because just a couple of years later, Fitbit purchased the company for nearly $40,000,000.

Loans: Small Business, Mortgage, Student, Automobile

An important part of your funding plan might include loans. It is very challenging for a person to pay cash for a home from the outset of their financial journey, so they finance a portion of their purchase using a home mortgage. When launching a small business or franchise, it might be necessary to obtain a commercial loan for a facility. Many people have utilized student loans to help them fund their educational dreams. Others have purchased their dream vehicle utilizing an automobile loan.

While I would highly discourage loans on anything that drops rapidly in value (like an automobile), some loans might make sense as part of your funding strategy. I personally obtained more than $20,000 in student loans when I attended Purdue University to study mechanical engineering from 1992 to 1996. I was able to repay the loans within eight years of my graduation. Although I am the youngest of six in my family, I became the first to graduate with a four-year degree. I began my engineering job the day following my graduation earning more than I ever dreamed of making. Within 8.5 years, my college debts were paid off, and my income had more than doubled. It was a worthwhile investment.

As my first small business venture grew, I had the opportunity to purchase a company generating five times more revenue than that of my own company. I brought on investors and was able to complete the purchase. Did I take risk? Absolutely! Would Dave Ramsey approve? Probably not! Did it work out? Absolutely. In fact, this single decision transformed my financial future forever. It has allowed me to accomplish far more than I ever thought possible with my personal finances. I'm also happy to share this particular company is debt free today, along with every other company I own.

Summary of Funding Sources

As you can tell, there are many options to consider when thinking through strategies for funding your dreams. Of course, these are just a few of the many possible options. Not all of them will be right for you. Be sure to explore the risks, challenges, stress, time, and energy that will be required for you to employ a particular funding method.

Some options, like utilizing your income from a job or second job, can be deployed right away and put to use quickly. Others, like stock investments or investing in a retirement account, will require deployment right away with the intention of utilizing them in a few decades.

The most important thing you can do right now is to prepare your dreams list, identify the potential funding sources you will utilize to pay for them, and *get started!* I shared a statement from Dave Ramsey earlier where he said, "Your most powerful wealth-building tool is your income…" He didn't stop there. He added an additional truth that will change your financial life substantially if you apply it long enough. Here is his entire statement: "Your most powerful wealth-building tool is your income until you get to the tipping point, where your investments earn more than you do."

Imagine this actually happening in your life: a time when your investments earn more than you do. At that moment, you could retire, or you could choose to dream again—and dream bigger.

Any dream you want to achieve beyond five years from today is ideal for funding by using the incredible power of compound interest through investments. If a $1,000 investment in a S&P 500 Index Fund grows at 11.40%[xiv] annually, it will be worth $1,763.52 in five years. That's a lot of money you didn't have to work for! Imagine if it were able to grow at the same compound annual growth for 40 years. The $1,000 investment will be worth $93,548.14. Amazing, isn't it?

When faced with funding an expensive dream, it is a natural thing for most people to say, "With my income, I can't afford that." This statement frustrates me! Of course, you can't afford most of your dreams straight out of your regular income. That's why you are reading this book — to find a way to fund them outside of your regular budget. Let me encourage you to strike the "I can't afford that" statement out of your vocabulary. Instead of saying, "I can't afford that," choose to ask, "*How* can I afford that?" Simply asking *how* will transform your thought process to consider funding options beyond your regular income. When a person first understands they do not have to work for every single dollar, it is a life-altering moment.

> When a person first understands they do not have to work for every single dollar, it is a life-altering moment.

Identify Funding Source(s) for each Dream

Now it is time to identify the potential funding source(s) for each of your dreams. Of course, longer term dreams can be less specific, but it is still important to plan for them too. Every one of your dreams needs at least one potential method matched with it.

Let me provide an example using a common dream: the dream of buying a home within the next couple of years. This is a Lifestyle Dream because it requires an acquisition cost (purchase

81

price of home plus closing costs), and it also has ongoing costs (mortgage payment, insurance, taxes, and utilities).

Knowing the type of dream and its costs, we can begin identifying the funding methods to employ to help it become reality. Let's consider the acquisition costs first. There are three acquisition costs: closing costs, down payment, and the difference between the purchase price and the down payment being made. For the down payment and closing costs, the funding methods include income from a regular job and a tax refund. The funding method for the remainder of the purchase price is a home mortgage loan from a bank. Once we've determined how to acquire the dream, let's consider how the ongoing costs, including utilities, homeowner's association fees, and general maintenance will be funded. This is a straight-forward decision since all of the ongoing costs can be funded from regular employment income.

Acquisition Costs	Funding Method
Closing Costs	Income from regular job
Down Payment	Income from regular job Plus my Tax Refund
Rest of Purchase Price	Mortgage loan from bank

Ongoing Costs	Funding Method
Utilities	Income from regular job
Annual HOA Fees	Income from regular job
Repairs Maintenance	Income from regular job

Download the Dreams List and other free resources at:
www.iwbnin.com/2020money

If this example makes sense to you, then the time has come for you to apply this funding process to each of your dreams. For your Moment Dreams, identify the funding methods you will use to pay for the acquisition costs. For all of your Lifestyle Dreams, be sure to identify the potential funding sources you will employ to pay for the ongoing costs in addition to the acquisition costs.

8

GET READY... GET SET... GO!

After reading all of this information about how to fund your dreams, it is easy to become overwhelmed and experience paralysis from the deluge of options and the challenges you face. Let me encourage you with this great passage written by Solomon and found in the book of Ecclesiastes.

Ecclesiastes 11:1-6
1 Ship your grain across the sea;
*   after many days you may receive a return.*
2 Invest in seven ventures, yes, in eight;
*   you do not know what disaster may come upon the land.*
3 If clouds are full of water,
*   they pour rain on the earth.*
Whether a tree falls to the south or to the north,
*   in the place where it falls, there it will lie.*
4 Whoever watches the wind will not plant;
*   whoever looks at the clouds will not reap.*
5 As you do not know the path of the wind,
*   or how the body is formed in a mother's womb,*
so you cannot understand the work of God,
*   the Maker of all things.*
6 Sow your seed in the morning,
*   and at evening let your hands not be idle,*
for you do not know which will succeed,
*   whether this or that,*
*   or whether both will do equally well.*

I find this passage to be both encouraging and challenging. While I could write another book discussing the depth of knowledge contained in these six verses, for the purposes of this book, let me call your attention to verse 4: Whoever watches the wind *will not plant*, whoever looks at the clouds *will not reap* (emphasis mine). Many people have paused in their pursuit of their dreams because of this very thing! They see the winds and clouds and mistakenly take them as signs that the time to move forward has not yet come. They wait for that blessed "perfect" time when they can see exactly how to accomplish every single part of their dream.

How often has the "perfect" time happened in your life? I had a dream to start an organization helping broke people improve their personal finances. While the Great Recession was an ideal time for people needing this sort of help, it was not the ideal time to quit a great job and lose the guarantee of salary and benefits! After all, a ton of people had *lost* their jobs and benefits, and I should have been holding on to mine with everything in me. But the time had arrived to step out into the unknown, to face the winds and clouds and pursue the dream.

Was it concerning to give up a set salary? Absolutely. Was it challenging to give up benefits like health insurance? Sure. But it didn't stop us from stepping out in faith. We purchased our own individual health insurance and chased the dream. As I write this book, the I Was Broke. Now I'm Not. team has just completed ten years of helping people win with their money. I am so grateful we took the steps of faith back then.

> Do *right now* what you'll look back at ten years from now and say, "I'm so glad I chose to do that back then!"

Let me encourage you to do the same. Do *right now* what you'll look back at ten years from now and say, "I'm so glad I chose to do that back then!"

A Detailed Example: Lisa's Dream House

Let's look at a practical example of someone with a short-term dream and how she went about funding it. Her name is Lisa, and she has always dreamed of home ownership. At age 28, she is ready to achieve her dream. This is a short-term dream, so it is important to clearly understand the actual costs as much as possible. As she looks at all of the homes located in her target area, Lisa discovers that her dream home has a price tag of $350,000. It is a four-bedroom home with 3.5 bathrooms. Her closing costs will be covered by the seller, and she is planning to pay a 5% down payment of $17,500. This will result in a monthly principal-and-interest payment of $1,685.[xv] As she reviews her dreams list, she correctly identifies this particular goal as a Lifestyle dream requiring an upfront acquisition cost plus ongoing costs.

With some research, she discovers the following regular ongoing financial commitments:

- Power: $250 per month (average)
- Natural Gas: $50 per month (average)
- Internet: $50 per month
- Homeowner's Insurance: $100 per month
- Property Taxes: $250 per month (paid annually)
- PMI: $80 per month
- Homeowner's Association: $100 per month

Additionally, Lisa wants to put money away for future home improvements and repairs. She estimates that saving $200 per month will be sufficient to cover most of these costs.

The ongoing regular costs total up to another $1,080 per month. This, plus the mortgage payment of $1,685, means Lisa will need $2,765 per month to fund her dream. This means the ongoing costs of her housing dream are $33,180 per year.

Lisa's pre-tax annual income is $60,000. From the $5,000 monthly gross salary, her take-home pay is $3,500. The monthly principal-and-interest payment alone of the home mortgage is nearly half of her take-home pay. When you include all of the proposed ongoing costs, the $2,765 will demand 79% of her take-home pay.

It is when faced with this type of challenge that most people will do something unthinkable: give up on their dream. They won't even fight for it!

"It's just too much money," they will say. They try to convince themselves further by adding, "It wasn't really my dream anyway."

There is a commonality between these two statements: they are both lies. Most people have said this at least once or twice in their lives. Knowing this, it is important to take a minute to think about these statements.

"It's just too much money." and *"It wasn't really my dream anyway."*

These are the most common reasons given by people who choose to stop pursuing a personal dream. Here is a fundamental truth: if a person will give up on a dream solely because they believe it costs too much, it wasn't really their dream in the first place. Think about Lisa's story. There are people who have spent more money on a *car* than she plans to spend on her home. I green-broke young racehorses as a teenager. I had the opportunity to take a filly to the famous Tattersalls Yearling Sale in Lexington, Kentucky. I saw far more than $350,000 being spent one horse. Many of them sold for more than $1 million!

My main point? There are millions of people who own houses costing $350,000 or more. If they can do it, Lisa can too.

How, you may ask? Is there a simple "snap your fingers and everything will magically work out" solution or perhaps a "buy it and the income will suddenly appear" type of approach?

Absolutely not. It will require something very challenging for most of us to do: think differently about money.

Robert Kiyosaki, the financial author, teacher, and real estate investor, shared a common problem with how most people view money when he shared what his dad taught him about money: "Go to school, get good grades, get a high-paying job..."[xvi]

All of this is good wisdom except for when it doesn't work! What about the person who didn't get good grades? What about the ones who got great grades but aren't hired for high-paying jobs? What if you received excellent grades and got a good job, but the salary still doesn't fund your dreams?

Are you supposed to do what millions of other people have done and just toss away your dreams because it costs too much? May it never be! Instead, lean into the challenge and choose to think differently about money.

Lisa is facing "The Gap." The Gap is the difference between what her current finances are able to afford and the actual price of her dream home. Most financial experts would recommend keeping the mortgage payment at 25% or less of her take-home pay. At her current income, this means her mortgage payment should be $875 or less. With her dream house mortgage payment of $1,685, Lisa's mortgage payment gap is $810.

It is also a general recommendation that the total monthly cost of home ownership equal 40% or less of her take-home income. Forty percent of Lisa's take-home pay is $1,400. With a total cost of home ownership totaling $2,765, the gap expands to $1,365 per month. If you have ever pursued a massive dream before, you know exactly how Lisa feels. She feels overwhelmed. It seems impossible. It is very tempting to just give up on the dream.

Lisa's feelings are natural because she is a human being. Most people have faced a time when a dream crashes into financial reality. Have you ever witnessed someone purchase something you thought was impossible and asked yourself, "How did he get the money for *that*?" Fill in the blank with the item or dream you saw him acquire. There is a good chance that the dream was funded by choosing to view finances differently from the general population.

Lisa has a decision to make:

- Option #1: She can attempt to find a creative way to fund the dream.
- Option #2: She can choose to forego the dream for now — pushing it off into the "1 to 5 years from now" category.
- Option #3: She can give up on the dream entirely.

When you face a financial challenge, you have the same options. Of course, Option #3 is the easiest and is what most people decide to do. They quit on their dream. What a pity!

Determining What to Do with Each Dream

When only looking at one dream at a time, it is difficult to make the best decision for what to do with each dream. This is because you won't always be able to see how funding one dream will affect all of the other ones. By thoroughly documenting all of your dreams on the Dreams Sheet and taking the time to consider their type (Moment or Lifestyle), calculate their associated costs, and plan their timing, you will be able to gain a full and complete view of your Fully Funded Life.

This allows you to see how a specific decision will affect all the funding and timing of all your other dreams. In most cases, it will make it easy for you to determine whether or not a particular decision is acceptable to you.

Of course, some dreams will require a lot more time to determine what is right for you. This is because some dreams can be mutually exclusive. If you have a dream to live full-time in Australia and the United States, it can be difficult to do this at the same time! Some people will have dreams their spouse does not agree with or support.

Many dreams will require more than just money to achieve. Other doors might need to open in order for you to pursue them. I live two hours away from Augusta, Georgia, the home of The Masters, the most famous golf tournament in the world. I have a dream of owning an official "Masters Badge" that would allow me to go to every round of the tournament without having to always go through a lottery process or rely on another badge holder. I know people who have gone decades without being selected in the lottery process. This dream will require more than money to achieve, but I plan to be ready if the opportunity presents itself!

As a kid, I dreamed of playing basketball for a living. Even at a height of 6′ 1″, I was able to slam dunk a basketball, but it turns out you need to be able to do much more than that to play in the NBA. My NBA dream ended early.

Other dreams may become impossible due to unforeseen circumstances. One of my dreams was to receive a piano lesson from the great pianist, Anthony Burger. His unfortunate passing at the age of 44 made my dream impossible. What a tremendous loss. This is why it is so important to pursue your dreams with great intention and focus. Even with focused intensity, you can still lose out on the opportunity to accomplish a dream. Knowing this, how many more opportunities will be lost if you choose to wander your way through life without a plan?

Lisa decided her dream fell into the "right now" category, so she started thinking of creative ways to fund her dream. With three spare bedrooms, she decided to rent out each one at a cost of $600 per month. The going rate of renting an apartment in her area is $900 per month, so $600 is a very attractive rate, meaning she should have little problems finding renters. In fact, within a few weeks, she signed rental contracts with three roommates.

With full occupancy, she will receive $1,800 per month in rent payments. Do you remember how much The Gap was for Lisa to fund each month? It was $1,365 — including utilities, taxes, PMI, insurance, and a $200 per month maintenance and repairs fee. This one decision allowed her to actually *lower* her total personal contribution from $2,765 to $965 meaning her total monthly contribution required is only 27.6% of her take-home pay.

With the decision made, Lisa purchased the home and is now living in her dream home—all while paying about the cost of an apartment.

Some people protest, "Lisa has to live with a bunch of people!" Others will agree, declaring, "I would never do that." It speaks to how much a person is willing to do to achieve their dream. Lisa wasn't willing to wait for the day when her income alone would sustain the dream, so she found a way to fund it sooner. Other people might prefer to wait until they can personally fund the entire dream because they are unwilling to deal with the challenges rentals can create. That's okay too!

Do not let others determine what is the wrong or right way to pursue your dreams. What is right for one person may be a totally wrong approach for another. Ultimately, you must live your life according to your God-given plans, hopes, and dreams. I have found the following two questions to be helpful when determining the steps you should take to fund your dreams.

1.   How far do you want to go?
2.   How fast do you need to get there?

How far do you want to go?

The scope of your Fully Funded Life will help you answer the total amount required to fund your dreams. When you add up all of your plans, hopes, and dreams that comprise your vision of a Fully Funded Life, how much money will it require? Is it a $1,000,000 set of dreams or will it take $100,000,000? Of course, we can't readily identify the costs to the exact penny, but this question should help you identify a rough overall amount.

Be sure to calculate both the acquisition cost and the ongoing amount required to sustain each dream. Your dreams might require $911,365 in acquisition costs while also creating an obligation of $7,131 in monthly ongoing costs. Knowing these two numbers is very helpful when preparing your funding plan.

Dreams with a total cost of $100,000,000 will require far different funding decisions than those costing $1,000,000. With giant dreams, you will need to focus on developing or acquiring a large investment portfolio of businesses, franchises, or real estate.

By the way, it is okay to be intimidated by the scope or cost of your dreams! If they were easy and straight-forward to accomplish, you would rely on your own strength. Always remember these are your God-given dreams. He gave them to you for a purpose. One of those purposes was to keep your focus upon him throughout your lifetime. Andraé Crouch, the great gospel singer and songwriter acknowledged this very thing when he wrote the following lyrics in his song *Through It All*: "For if I never had a problem, I wouldn't know that God could solve them."

There will be times along your journey when you will experience what you view as a setback. When faced with such a challenge, it is easy to say, "Why did this happen to me?" I would venture to say that nearly every single human in history has asked this question at some point in his or her life. I was inspired when I watched Dr. Elijah Cummings, Maryland's 7th District United States House of Representatives member, speak on Capitol Hill with someone facing legal issues. He said, "...I tell my children, I say when bad things happen to you, do not ask the question why did it happen *to* me? Ask the question, why did it happen *for* me?"[xvii]

Anthony Burger was using a baby walker at eight months old and fell into a heating duct on the floor of his house, receiving third-degree burns on his face, legs, and hands. Burger's doctors told his parents that was likely to not be able to move his hands in the future. God had other plans. At age five, Anthony was recognized as a piano prodigy. His gift allowed him to receive the Singing News Award "Instrumentalist of the Year" ten times — an award since renamed "The Anthony Burger Award" because of his prodigious talent.

Dave Ramsey built a real estate portfolio worth more than $4 million, much of it with short-term debt. A call on his loans led to a financial collapse. Instead of wondering why this happened to him, he set out to learn from the challenges. Millions of people have advanced in their personal finances because Dave decided to share his learnings via a radio show, books, live events, and classes.

The fact that you are reading this book and have made it to this point tells me you have big dreams yet to be funded. As you encounter the challenges of facing the great distance you still have to go, view each obstacle as a preparatory step helping you advance along your journey.

How fast do you need to get there?

This helps you answer the timing question. Lisa wanted to fund her dream immediately. This required the down payment as an acquisition cost, and it also demanded she secure three renters right away. Had she chosen to delay her dream, the acquisition cost might have increased, but she would have been able to avoid having to find renters too.

If you have a lot of time to fund a particular dream, it will provide more flexibility in the methods that can be employed. More time usually equals more options. Less time usually demands more creativity and provides fewer funding methods.

Travis had a dream of flying his bride back to the tropical islands where they had honeymooned ten years earlier. Because his dream was timed with his tenth anniversary, he had less than a year to figure out how to fund it. As he looked at potential ways to fund his dream, it was clear that his regular income didn't have the ability to pay for it in such a short timeframe. He was committed to incur zero debt from this special trip, so credit cards weren't a viable option. Travis had to be creative and utilize skill sets he already possessed.

One skill set and hobby he enjoyed was trucks — especially four-wheel drive vehicles and SUVs. From time to time, he had even bought and sold a used vehicle to make some extra money. He decided to focus on this as his funding method. Over the course of a few months, he bought and sold several used vehicles and earned enough money to pay cash for their all-inclusive weeklong adventure!

It is amazing how a short time window and an urgent dream will result in innovation and propels people to fund a dream they would have never believed possible a few months prior. You've probably experienced this in your own life. A dream really does set the eyes agleam.

Once you have determined how fast you need to go and how soon you need to get there, it is time to chase those dreams.

Get ready... Get set... Go!

9

INITIATING MOVEMENT TOWARD FUNDING YOUR VISION

An old Chinese proverb talks about the importance of getting started: "A journey of a thousand miles begins with a single step." As I shared earlier, I have run two full marathons. Full marathons require the runner to complete a course measuring 26.2 miles. I began the journey to complete each race with a single step. As I stood alongside thousands of other runners at the starting line, I could have given up, saying to myself, "I'm slower than a lot of these runners. Why bother?" Instead, I focused on my personal time goal and took my first step. As I ran, momentum helped power me along. Two hundred twenty-seven minutes later, I chugged across the finish line, elated for accomplishing my dream. It would not have happened if I had allowed the challenge to paralyze me before I took my first step. It's time for you to take a step toward your dreams.

As you review your dreams and the funding method you've identified for each one, think about what you can do *right now* or *right away* to initiate movement for them to become reality.

Do you need to open an investment account to prepare for funding of your retirement dreams? Perhaps you need to sign up for a real estate investing class or conference. Maybe it is time to purchase some books focused on helping you launch your new business. It might be time to go back to school to get an entirely new degree or certification. If you're interested in owning a franchise, it might make sense to search Google and figure out how to contact your preferred franchise provider and begin the process of becoming an owner.

The key is to get started *right away*. Delayed dreams and lack of progress can be joy-robbing and lead to complete paralysis where months or years go by without moving forward. Proverbs 13:4 shares this great wisdom: "A sluggard's appetite is never filled, but the desires of the diligent are fully satisfied." Why is the sluggard's appetite never filled? It's because their lack of diligence has resulted in zero progress and produced nothing for them. The diligent are fully satisfied because the Lord makes their work profitable. Proverbs 21:5 attests to this truth: "The plans of the diligent lead to profit as surely as haste leads to poverty." Those who have a plan and are diligent will be rewarded with a profit.

On Sunday, May 12, 1996, I graduated from Purdue University. The very next day I was scheduled to begin my first full-time engineering job. At my graduation, one of my brothers put his hands on my shoulders and said, "Joe! Tomorrow you will start your new job. Go straight to Human Resources and tell them to max out your contribution to the company retirement plan—the 401(k)." The next morning, I went to Human Resources and did as my brother had strongly suggested. While I don't remember a lot of the conversation, I do remember that the lady was somewhat confused by my request because apparently very few employees were contributing that much to their own retirement accounts.

Here is the lesson. I made a decision on that day and took a step. It was the beginning of a multi-decade journey to retirement.

Much like taking my first step to complete a marathon, it got me started toward the finish line. Now, more than twenty years later, I'm so glad I took that first step!

Once you've sought the Lord and taken the time to document all your plans, hopes, and dreams, it is time to focus your efforts on the steps necessary to accomplish them. As Paul wrote in Colossians 3:23-24: "Whatever you do, work at it with all your heart, as working for the Lord, not for human masters, since you know that you will receive an inheritance from the Lord as a reward. It is the Lord Christ you are serving."

You do not need to know the entire pathway to accomplishing your goal. There are some things that will require God to make a way for it to become possible. Perhaps this is why the author wrote in Psalm 119:105, "Your word is a lamp for my feet, a light on my path." The lamp for our feet allows us to clearly see our next step and provides some illumination for the path ahead. It doesn't promise to show you all the way to the achievement of your dreams. Take the next step, even though you may not clearly see the entire way.

Have you ever driven in thick fog? If you have, you know it can cause traffic to move at a snail's pace or maybe even bring it to a full stop. I have observed something interesting about driving in heavy fog: I can always see at least a few feet ahead. When I move forward, I can still see a few feet ahead. The clarity moves with me! One thing I know for sure is that if I keep moving, there will be a time when all the fog lifts and the sun will break through, allowing me to once again race forward at full speed.

You will surely have similar moments as you move toward your dreams. In fact, you probably have several dreams right now where the path forward isn't really clear. What should you do — stop moving altogether or move forward slowly and cautiously with small steps? Can I encourage you to take those small steps? If you do, there will surely be a day where 20/20 clarity will burst forth, and you will be able to race toward the accomplishment of your dream!

Let me share an example. Rose has a dream of retiring one day with $1 million in her retirement accounts. She is 35 years old and has not yet saved anything toward this goal. She read *I Was Broke. Now I'm Not.* and began her climb up the I Was Broke. Now I'm Not. Ladder. She quickly accomplished Rungs #1 (Set Goals) and #2 (Save money — start with one month of expenses), and now she is facing Rung #3 — "Invest enough to capture full company match (or $100/month — whichever is greater)." Her employer doesn't have a retirement account available and will not match any retirement fund contributions. As she looks over her budget, Rose decides to eliminate her cable bill ($100/month) and redirect it toward investments into her Roth IRA retirement account. Her desired retirement age is 67 so she currently has 32 years to reach her goal.

With a monthly investment of $100 per month for the next 32 years, Rose will be able to make substantial progress toward her goal of $1 million. Without any growth, Rose will have saved $38,400. However, invested in an S&P 500 index fund and growth at the rate it has averaged since 1941 (11.4% compounded annual growth rate), this modest contribution will grow to $386,760.85. It's not one million dollars, but it is way more than zero! It will move her a long way toward her giant, mega-sized goal!

After one year, Rose will pay off her car and free up her monthly car payment of $341.06. She decides to use a little over half of the newly liberated car payment money to boost her retirement contribution. An additional $180 per month brings her total monthly investment to $280. Over the first year of investing $100 per month, her account will grow to $1,264.73. Of these funds, $1,200 is from her contributions and $64.73 is from growth. With 31 years remaining to achieve her retirement goal and an increased contribution of $280 per month, Rose will end up contributing a total of $105,360 to her retirement dream. However, with compounded annual growth of 11.4%, her retirement account will grow to $1,006,225.70 by age 67. The Lord-willing, Rose will achieve her massive dream. It will happen because she dared to dream and resolved to take her first step.

What will happen if Rose prepares her plan and completes all of the fun math exercises but then chooses to do nothing for five years? She will make zero progress toward her retirement dream. If she waits five years to start, she will have "only" $601,313.95. It is still a lot of money, but it is far less than the $1 million she could have accumulated. In fact, Rose would have to invest $469 per month for 27 years, a total of $151,956, to make up the difference. This is why it is so vitally important to start *right away.*

Many people freeze up when they face substantial challenges to their dreams. This is especially true when the challenge is financial in nature. Let me remind you that God owns the cattle on a thousand hills (Psalm 50:10). He can sell a few for you but not if you are lazy. Laziness and lack of knowledge have cost many people dearly. Don't add your name to the list.

> Laziness and lack of knowledge have cost many people dearly. Don't add your name to the list.

Put Key Tasks and Milestones on Your Calendar

What are the key tasks you need to complete in order to achieve your dream? If real estate is part of your funding plan, find the classes, conferences, and mastermind group meetings you need to attend. Register for them and put the dates on your calendar. You might feel overwhelmed because you're totally new to this, but that's okay. These feelings will go away as you gain knowledge and find people, some of whom will probably become your future mentors, who have been highly successful doing for decades what you're preparing to do for the first time.

If a stock or mutual fund investment is part of your funding strategy, when will you set up your trading account? Put the date on your calendar. Better yet, open the trading account right now! If you are overwhelmed when faced with the question, "What type of account would you like to open: IRA, Roth IRA, or Trading Account?" set up an appointment with an investment advisor to help you make the right choice.

Deadlines move people to accomplish things. I once saw a quote addressing this very thing. It said, "If it weren't for last minutes, half of the world's work would never get done." Set a deadline for each activity to initiate movement toward establishment and achievement of your funding methods.

Is a small business going to be one of your funding methods? Set a deadline for when you will complete your business plan. Set another date for when you want the business to begin operating. Put these important milestones and dates on your calendar and hold yourself accountable to them.

SMART Goals

Many people have been able to make huge progress by following the SMART Goal methodology. Each letter stands for a word that provides a framework for setting good goals.

- **S –** Specific: The more specific the goal, the more clearly you will know whether or not you are making progress.
- **M –** Measurable: There must be a way to measure whether or not a goal is being achieved.
- **A –** Attainable: There should be a reasonable chance a particular goal is actually possible.
- **R –** Relevant: Of course, the goal should be directly related to the accomplishment of your plans, hopes, and dreams.
- **T –** Timebound: There is nothing like a deadline to drive key goals to completion.

Let's look at an example of a goal through the SMART framework. Suppose a fisherman named Bob has a dream of owning a fishing boat which can also be used as a ski boat. It will cost $30,000. Bob could write down his goal this way: "I want to own a fishing boat which can also be used as a ski boat."

Does Bob's goal meet the standards of a SMART goal? Let's analyze it using each word.

- **S**pecific: Bob's goal is somewhat specific. It could be more specific if the goal included a brand name of the boat, length, boat motor size, brand name of the motor, and other details. However, it is a decent start toward being specific. RATING: 75%

- **M**easurable: It is definitely measurable. Bob will either have a fishing boat that can also be used as a ski boat, or he will not have one. RATING: 100%
- **A**ttainable: It is an attainable goal. There are millions of boats, and there's certainly a great chance his name could be on one someday. RATING: 100%
- **R**elevant: It is absolutely relevant to Bob's goals. RATING: 100%
- **T**imebound: Is there a deadline mentioned in his goal? Nope. This is where many goals fail because without a deadline, it is open-ended and could drag on perpetually. RATING: 0%

Let's see if we can improve his written goal so it will meet all five parts of the SMART goal framework. What if he wrote his goal this way?

"I want to own an 18-foot Tracker Pro-Guide V-175 Combo boat with a Mercury 90-hp FourStroke motor by the end of this year."

By applying the five parts of the SMART methodology, we've greatly improved Bob's goal by making it more specific and establishing a clear deadline for its accomplishment.

Look at each of your goals through the SMART lens and see if this will help improve your progress toward each one. No matter your goals, it is important to get started toward them right away. Remember, you only get one life. Live it well and fully devoted toward the plans, hopes, and dreams God has placed in your heart.

10

SUSTAINING PROGRESS TOWARD YOUR FULLY FUNDED LIFE

"Without continual growth and progress, such words as improvement, achievement, and success have no meaning." Although these words were written by Benjamin Franklin many years ago, they are just as relevant today as ever. Once you have taken time to prepare a funding plan for each of your dreams and initiated movement toward each one, it is important to sustain your progress. This is where the biggest challenge lies— maintaining progress over great lengths of time.

Steve was a young child in school. One day, his teacher gave the class a writing assignment. They were to write about what they wanted to be when they grew up. Steve wrote about his dream of being on television. His teacher rejected it, told him his dream was unrealistic, and forced him to rewrite it. When Steve came home and told his mother, she told him to do as his teacher had instructed and write down another dream. Because it was truly Steve's dream, he was not very willing to listen to his mother. His father heard the commotion and thought his son was disobeying his mother. Any father who has had a child disrespect his or her mother knows the special feelings this creates!

Steve's dad, known to everyone as Slick, went into the room to deal with the situation. Upon discovering that the teacher was trying to get Steve to abandon his dream, Slick did something extraordinary. He asked, "What's wrong with that?" Steve's father was questioning why it was a problem to dream of being on television. With his question, he taught Steve two very important things. First, he taught him that it was okay to dream. Second, Slick demonstrated that he was *for* his son's dream of being on TV.

After taking some time to talk about it with Steve's mother, Slick came in to meet with Steve. Steve believed he was going to receive "a whoopin'," in his words, for causing trouble with his teacher and mother. Instead, Slick asked Steve what he thought the teacher wanted him to write. Steve shared that the teacher wanted him to write what all the other kids were writing—things like being a basketball player or something similar to that.

Slick responded, "Well, put that on the paper. Take that to school tomorrow and give it to her. Take your paper (the one with his dream of being on TV) and put it in your drawer. Every morning when you get up, read your paper. And every night before you go to bed, read your paper. That's your paper."

Today, Steve Harvey is a runaway success in television. He refused to allow another person to squash his dream. In fact, while his teacher was still living, he sent her a brand-new television every year for Christmas just to be sure she could see him.

When Steve would see his teacher, she would say, "Boy, you send me all these TVs from wherever you are, and you don't understand. I got too many TVs. I have to give these TVs away sometimes."

"I know. It's alright though," said Steve.

He continued by saying, "And I kept that paper, and that little boy with the stuttering problem is on television, seven days a week. Yeah, I'm on TV. All the time."[xviii]

There will be times where you encounter challenges to accomplishing your dreams. People will doubt you. There will be financial obstacles. Many things will compete for your time. There will be times when you simply don't know what your next step should be.

It is in the crucible of these challenges that you might be inclined to modify your dream or give up entirely. However, when viewed through the right lens, it is also a time when you will prove that your dream really is *your* dream. This 20/20 vision will provide extra energy and grant the perseverance to stick with it.

Steve could have listened to this major influencer in his life, his teacher, and allowed her to change his dream. After all, it's one thing for a random stranger to shoot down your dreams; it's quite another when it's someone you admire. Instead, he chose to use her words as fuel to propel him forward. Steve had the blessing of a father who chose to hear his son's dream and help him believe in it. I wonder what would have happened if he hadn't received such positive reinforcement at home? He may have given up on his dream right then and there. There is a lot we can learn from Steve's story.

Let's consider some strategies to help you sustain progress and momentum even when you face difficult challenges. By employing these techniques and tips, you will position yourself to make tremendous progress toward your Fully Funded Life even as you face adversity.

Receive negative words as a challenge instead of a putdown

Other people will always have an opinion about what you should do. When they choose to share their doubts about your dream, don't receive it is as a putdown, even if they intend it that way. If you get caught up in their negativity, you will focus too much energy on feelings like anger or resentment. Instead, use the words as jet fuel for your journey. Many great things have been accomplished because someone was told he or she couldn't do something!

Steve Harvey harnessed the power of his teacher's words and converted an event that could have ended his dream into a launching pad for his future.

Michael Jordan used the event of being cut from the team to drive himself to practice more and improve his game. As a fan who grew up watching Michael play, I am so glad he didn't receive the cut as the final judgment of his ability to play basketball.

Susan Boyle was toiling through life, but her real passion was singing. She stuck with it until her moment arrived on Britain's Got Talent. When she sang, "I Dreamed a Dream" from Les Misérables, all the world knew that a new star was born right before their eyes. How did she end up on the show's stage that night? It was because she persevered and continued to take next steps.

Steve Jobs was fired from Apple Computer, the company he started in 1985. Talk about a punch to the gut! In spite of the very public nature of his departure, he chose to embrace the challenge in a positive and productive manner by pursuing his next dream: a new computer company which was appropriately named NeXT. He then went on to found Pixar, bringing its first computer-animated film, *Toy Story*, to the masses. In 1997, just twelve short years later, Apple merged with NeXT and Steve soon became CEO of Apple again. His perseverance affected nearly every person living on earth as Apple, under his visionary leadership, produced the iPod, iPad, and iPhone.

Look at any successful person who is actively living a Fully Funded Life and accomplishing big dreams, and you will see a person who has overcome many naysayers. They have been able to use those negative words as fuel to propel themselves forward.

Surround yourself with positive and encouraging people

When you encounter challenges in the pursuit of your Fully Funded Life, it is wonderful to have fellow dreamers walking alongside you. Their encouragement will provide a positive balance to help you navigate the negative people, financial setbacks, and other things that can cause discouragement while moving toward your goal.

Steve Harvey had such a person in his father. As a father myself, I take particular interest in Slick's approach with his son. Instead of becoming outraged and demanding a parent-teacher conference, he chose a low-key approach. Through his actions, he was really saying, "Son, do what you need to do to make the teacher happy, but this is so much bigger than a writing assignment. You can keep your dream."

If he didn't know it before then, Steve learned through this challenge that he had someone in his corner. You need people in your corner too. Who is on your side? Think about the people you spend the most time with in your daily life. Are they positive? Do they encourage others? Do they help propel you toward your dream?

It is important to recognize that these people are not "yes" people, approving everything you do without ever providing accountability. As you progress toward your dream, you want to have people who will challenge you too. When they see you veer off-course, they will say something. If you do something dumb, they will not hesitate to say, "That was dumb. Why did you do that?" Of course, because they are positive and encouraging, they will follow up with an affirmation like, "You've got this. Come on! Let me help you."

Write down your dream. Look at your dream. Review your dream.

I'm confident you've now written down many of your plans, hopes, and dreams. It is important not to "check it off" as an activity you have completed. Your dreams list needs to be a living and active document to be reviewed on a regular basis. As you make progress toward each dream and your Fully Funded Life, be sure to add new ones to the list. After all, as you accomplish more with your life, you will surely be exposed to new and exciting opportunities, people, events, and places. Put them on the list. As the saying goes, "Variety is the spice of life."

There have been periods in my life where I've gone months without looking at my dreams list. Life happened. We got busy. Children showed up. Guess what happened when a lot of time went by without reviewing my dreams? We made a lot less progress.

If you're not intentional, years can go by without reviewing your dreams. Use technology to help you stay the course. I have a reminder established on my calendar that says, "Review dreams list with Jenn." It is set to remind me with a pop-up note every three months. We may not immediately review our dreams at the exact time the reminder shows up, but it triggers the establishment of a discussion focused on our dreams.

I have found it helpful to have a system for reviewing my plans, hopes, and dreams. I'm going to give you a place to start and then once you get a good rhythm, feel free to modify it to make it work the best for you. As a married couple with young children still in the house, we have found that this is best done in the context of a date day or night without children present. If you are single, you might find it helpful to review your dreams with a mentor or fellow dreamer who is actively making progress toward his or her dreams.

Fully Funded Life Dreams Review (90 minutes)

1. **Review your dreams list along with their timing.** (10 mins) This should be a brief review of each dream. It is helpful to say them out loud as it makes each one more tangible and real to you.
2. **Identify progress toward each dream.** (10 mins) It is easy to focus on negatives. Avoid this. Instead, identify progress you have made toward your dreams and write it down.
3. **Celebrate the progress made.** (10 mins) High-five. Hug. Kiss. Fist-bump. Cheer. Whatever you do to celebrate, do it! You are making progress toward your dreams, and it is worth taking time to recognize the results of your efforts.
4. **Identify any setbacks experienced for individual dreams.** (20 mins) Identify the reasons for the setbacks. Are there any things that could have been avoided? What changes are necessary to get back on track?
5. **Make adjustments as necessary.** (20 mins) Determine the steps that will help you make progress toward your Fully

Funded Life. It is this process of refinement that will ensure you make continued progress toward your dreams.

6. **Add new dreams to the list**. (20 mins) Are there any new dreams you need to add to your list? Consider both Moment and Lifestyle Dreams.

7. **Pray**. (as long as you like) Philippians 4:6 shares this wisdom, "Do not be anxious about anything, but in every situation, by prayer and petition, with thanksgiving, present your requests to God." This is wonderful guidance for life!

Track Your Net Worth Quarterly.

Since nearly every dream comes with a cost, it is important to keep track of your financial progress. Not all financial investments generate monthly income, so measuring your net worth is an excellent way to determine whether or not you are making progress toward funding each of your goals.

For instance, suppose a couple purchased a rental house with a fifteen-year mortgage to help fund their child's college education. The child was two years old when they bought the rental. They recognized that most, if not all, of the rental income during the fifteen year pay off period will be used to repay the mortgage and cover necessary repairs. This does not, however, mean they will not make any progress toward their dream of funding college.

While some of their monthly payment is interest paid to their lender, a substantial portion of it is transferring into home equity. In an ideal scenario, the home will increase in value during the repayment period. A net worth calculation allows the family to actually see the total equity gained and encourages them during their journey to fund their dream.

Suppose the family acquired the rental home for $131,578.95. They paid a 5% down payment of $6,578.95 and borrowed $125,000 for 15 years at a fixed rate of 4%. Their monthly payment is $924.61. They receive rent sufficient to cover the payment plus taxes, insurance, and general repairs. Imagine their thoughts when they calculated their net worth at the end the first year of ownership and discover that their equity of $6,578.95 (their down payment) has now grown to $12,787.26 due to the principal balance being reduced with each payment made! Suppose the house also grows in value at a modest rate of 1% annually. Think about how they felt at the end of year number eight when they realized that the home's value had increased from $131,578.95 to $141,070.44 and their total equity in the home was now $73,426.65. That would already cover a lot of college bills for their child who, by the way, was still eight years away from enrolling in college.

Let's look at their net worth situation when the child finally turns eighteen and prepares to attend college. Since the mortgage term was fifteen years, the home is completely paid off. Its value has grown to $152,759. With the home paid off, they have liberated the $924.61 monthly mortgage payment and been able to put $700 of the monthly rent collection into their savings account each month. These calculations do not even include rent increases that may have been implemented during their sixteen years of ownership.

Do you see the power of measuring your net worth on a consistent basis? If you are not careful, you will only see the cash leaving each and every month. Measuring your net worth allows you to see the real financial story and can provide much needed encouragement along the way toward funding your dream.

Allow Financial Mentors to Speak into Your Life.

Recently, I was listening to a news anchor talk about the results of a soccer match. In an unusual turn of events, one team scored a lot of goals against the other team during a major match and won with a final score of 13-0. "That's a lot of points," he said. When the news anchor said the word *points,* I immediately knew he didn't know much about soccer. No one with any soccer knowledge would say points. They would say the proper term: goals.

When it comes to sustaining your journey toward a Fully Funded Life, it is important to have financial mentors who know what they are talking about. Proverbs 15:22 shares this great wisdom: "Plans fail for lack of counsel, but with many advisers, they succeed."

If you are going to choose rental real estate as one of your methods for funding your dreams, be sure to have financial mentors who have a lot of experience in the area of rental real estate. Interested in starting a small business to help fund several dreams? Make sure you have a network of business leaders who have successfully launched their own small business. If you are going to choose investments in the stock market as your preferred financial vehicle for funding your dreams, obtain advice from professional investment advisers.

While it is helpful to like your financial mentors, it is more important that they know what they are talking about and can help you advance toward your personal goals. Some of these advisers will charge you money for their wisdom. That's okay. Consider your answer to two questions. First, if they can help you avoid costly errors and mistakes, would it be a worthwhile investment to pay for their advice? Secondly, if they will help you achieve your Fully Funded Life, would it be a worthwhile investment to pay for their help?

Proverbs 4:7 would certainly say "Yes!" to each of these questions. This verse says, "The beginning of wisdom is this: Get wisdom. Though it cost all you have, get understanding." I smile every time I read this verse because the first part is so funny. "The beginning of wisdom is this: Get wisdom." It is stating the obvious. It is common sense, yet the majority of people fail to do it when it comes to money. They try to do it all by themselves. As the old quote goes, "Common sense has become so uncommon that it is almost like a superpower."

It is the second part of Proverbs 4:7 that has made a huge impact on my ability to live a Fully Funded Life. "Though it cost <u>all</u> you have, get understanding." I emphasize "all" because this is a very high cost. Why would the writer say it is worth spending *all you have* to get wisdom? Because he knew wisdom attracts wealth and helps a person gain the ability to accomplish his or her God-given plans, hopes, and dreams.

Based on your own financial strategies, what type of financial wisdom do you need to invite into your journey toward a Fully Funded Life? Be willing to pay for it, if necessary!

Build and Fiercely Protect Financial Margin.

In order to sustain progress toward your dreams, it is critically important to build financial margin and fiercely protect it along the way. Make no mistake about it, one of the primary ways people's journeys toward Fully Funded Lives are derailed is an ongoing lack of saved money. A person without financial margin will continually be distracted from his calling and mission because he must deal with financial challenges created by regular life events. Without saved money, a simple car breakdown can cause great stress and cause a person to lose focus for a week or more. That is a huge price to pay for a simple car breakdown.

As I teach in my book, *I Was Broke. Now I'm Not.*, it is important to follow the I Was Broke. Now I'm Not. Ladder process. It will help you build and protect financial margin which ultimately allows you to protect your progress toward a Fully Funded Life. Rung #2 is focused on building an emergency fund large enough to cover an entire month of expenses. Rung #5 is all about increasing your hedge of protection to a minimum of three months of expenses.

Think about your high school English teacher for a minute. Do you remember when your teacher would ruin your life by making you write a two-page term paper? She would then increase the pain by forcing you to actually hand-write the paper. As if that wasn't enough, she would issue the ultimate heartbreak by demanding you write it single-spaced. Usually, she would give one final instruction: "Be careful not to write in the *margins*." What are the margins? It is the space along the edge of the paper. Maybe this is why saved money is called "financial *margin*." This financial margin creates *space* for life to happen and prevents distractions from impeding your pursuit of a Fully Funded Life.

You may have noticed I wrote a very strong word in this tip: *fiercely*. I have used this word on purpose because you will experience events that require intense effort to protect your savings account. You will have to defend your savings from all sorts of assaults. Your children will come home crying because all of their friends have a possession (like a video game console, phone, bike, doll, etc.). They will tell you how it is not fair for them "to be the only person in the world without one." Don't use your savings, the margin you have fought to build, to buy it for them.

Your car will break down *again*, tempting you to purchase a new one and finance it for six years. What if the new car requires you to use your savings for the down payment? What if the monthly payment for the next six years costs you the ability to fund the dream of paying for your children's college? Fix up the old car and drive it proudly knowing you have protected financial margin which will preserve your progress toward a Fully Funded Life.

After speaking together at a conference, I had the opportunity to ride to the airport with noted leadership guru and author, Dr. John C. Maxwell. He had heard my talk on personal finances and shared something his father had told him: "John, you can choose to either play now and pay later, or you can pay now and play later. The choice is yours." At that moment, I realized my actions had already revealed my choice: I was paying *now* so I could play later.

Whatever the challenge you face, if it requires you to erode financial margin or prevents you from moving toward your Fully Funded Life, it isn't worth it. You won't always have to make such tough decisions, by the way. By choosing to sacrifice right now, you will position yourself to live a Fully Funded Life later.

Make your goals (and your progress toward funding them) visual.

When you have many different goals, it is difficult to fully comprehend your progress toward funding each one of them when you are just looking at the numbers on a spreadsheet or reviewing your bank account balance. Even calculating your net worth only allows you to see progress in numbers and charts. When we were paying off our debt, it was difficult to really see our progress until we came up with a way to visually track our progress.

As we were looking at our home mortgage balance, we said, "Wow! That is a lot of debt. Paying this house off is like trying to eat an elephant!" We remembered the old question, "How do you eat an elephant?" The answer? "One bite at a time." This inspired a solution for tracking our goal progress. I created a rough drawing of our house floor plan on the computer and put a bunch of squares in it. I was able to fit 2,426 squares into the outline. I divided the price of the home ($174,900) by the number of squares (2,426) to calculate a value for each square ($72.14). We titled it the "Sangl Home Pay-off Spectacular" because I loved the ridiculousness of it.

With this one simple step, we transformed a huge goal into bite-sized pieces. For every $72.14 we paid off in principal, we were able to color in a square. While it might seem like a really simple idea, it was unbelievable how much it allowed us to actually *see* our progress! It was a massive accomplishment when we were able to finish paying off this house exactly 72 months after we purchased it. Now, as I reflect on this huge achievement for our family, I realize the real fun was actually the *journey* of paying it off. Every single month, we focused on how we might be able to pay off just one more square than the previous month. It made us such better money managers. I suspect the same will be true for you and your family.

Sangl Home Pay-off Spectacular

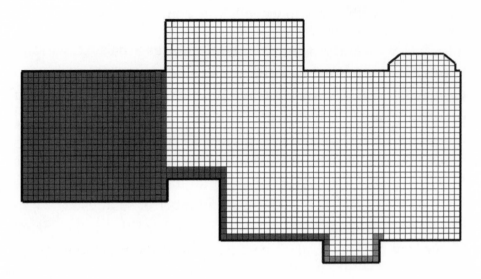

Why not utilize this idea to track your progress toward funding your dreams? Do you dream of going to Italy? A "Dream Trip to Italy" savings spectacular will allow you to visually track your progress toward it. Maybe you dream of owning a John Deere tractor. I'm certain a "John Deere" savings spectacular will be fun to color in as you fund it. Just be sure to use a green marker. There is a really good chance you will not have to create your own "spectacular" as we have more than one hundred of them at www.iwbnin.com/spectacular—all ready and prepared for you to begin visually tracking your own journey to fund each of your dreams.

There is an added bonus when you begin visually tracking your progress toward your goal: it is more likely to be reviewed on a consistent basis. If you place your spectaculars on the refrigerator, it will spark conversations with your family and friends. This will allow you to share your dreams as well as enable you to invite them into your journey.

118

Hold your dreams loosely.

One of the biggest mistakes many of us make is to try and control every single aspect of our lives and dreams. This is a mistake for several reasons, but the biggest one is because it is an impossible task! Great wisdom is found in Proverbs 19:21: "Many are the plans in a person's heart, but it is the Lord's purpose that prevails."

When you find it challenging to pursue a particular dream, keep your eyes open for what the Lord might be preparing for you next. It was my dream to be CEO of a large publicly traded company. Even as I climbed the ladder rapidly, I realized God was calling me to leave corporate America and enter into full-time ministry at a church I had helped plant. This did not line up with my dreams at all. However, when I realized it was his purpose for my life, it gave me the strength to exchange my dream for God's calling.

I'm so glad I held my dream loosely. I was able to be a part of NewSpring Church in Anderson, South Carolina, as it grew from just 15 people meeting in a farmhouse to more than 30,000 in attendance each weekend! I had no idea my ministry position was God's way of preparing me to lead INJOY Stewardship Solutions, an organization that helps churches raise funds for major projects like building a new sanctuary, children's facility, or family life center. My CEO dream came true, but in a role far different than I ever imagined. It is very rewarding.

It reminds me of the second most popular verse in the Bible, Jeremiah 29:11, "'For I know the plans I have for you,' declares the Lord, 'plans to prosper you and not to harm you, plans to give you hope and a future.'" God has a way of directing our paths even when life doesn't seem to make any sense.

You have probably experienced similar events in your life. You most definitely will face more in the future. Whenever it happens, just smile and say, "I can't wait to see what you're going to do next, God."

Become Debt-Free.

Debt freedom is one of the greatest ways to ensure you can stay focused on pursuing your dreams. If you've achieved debt freedom, you know how amazing it feels and what it allows you to do. When there are no car payments, zero credit card debt, and you don't owe anyone money, you free up your income to pursue even greater dreams. I'll never forget the day my family achieved debt freedom. When we started our journey in December 2002, we had four major debts: a home mortgage, truck loan, credit card debt, and student loans.

The truck loan, credit card debt, and student loans were our first targets because they were all part of Rung #4 of the I Was Broke. Now I'm Not. Ladder: "Eliminate all non-house, non-business debt." Utilizing the debt snowball technique, we paid off these debts in just 14 months! This allowed us to use the money that previously went to payments to speed up our progress toward funding dreams. It was like a supercharger. In January 2013, just ten years and one month after we began our debt freedom journey, we achieved Rung #7: "Pay off house and business debt" when we were able to pay off our home mortgage.

If accomplishing Rung #4 was like supercharging our plans, hopes, and dreams, then achieving Rung #7 was like attaching a rocket to them. It was a pivotal time in our life. We're not alone or unique. Millions have prioritized debt freedom and experienced far more than financial freedom. They've been able to purchase freedom from a lot of stress and anxiety and gained confidence to pursue the bigger dreams in their lives.

Calculating your debt freedom date is easy when you use the Debt Freedom Date Calculator located in the "Tools" section of www.iwbnin.com. Making the decision to become debt-free is difficult. However, it is the *work* of becoming debt-free and sticking to good financial decisions for months and years that is most challenging. Many people begin the journey to debt freedom, but after a few months they encounter a financial challenge and revert back to the very financial decisions that led to debt in the past.

If you want to give your plans, hopes, and dreams the best chance for success, choose to pursue debt freedom, at least at the Rung #4 level, having no debt except for a home mortgage. You will be so glad you did.

Practice Contentment Continually.

One of the greatest challenges for driven people is maintaining an attitude of contentment. When you have a list of dreams and feel thousands of miles away from living a Fully Funded Life, it can be very easy to fall into the trap of self-pity, anger, and frustration. If you are not careful, this can easily spawn other terrible things like greed and selfishness.

The Apostle Paul wrote in I Timothy 6:6, "But godliness with contentment is great gain." This is a powerful truth. Godliness coupled with contentment is great gain. However, the opposite is not always true. Great gain is not always godly nor does it guarantee contentment! As has been said by many people, more stuff won't bring happiness if one is not grounded in his or her faith and consistently focused on maintaining an "attitude of gratitude."

As the late great Zig Ziglar famously said, "Money won't make you happy, but everyone wants to find out for themselves." We all believe our own experience with wealth would never have the negative challenges others have faced. Jesus spoke about this very thing when he said in Luke 12:15, *"Watch out! Be on your guard against all kinds of greed; life does not consist in an abundance of possessions."*

Paul found contentment in his journey because of his relationship with the Lord. He shared a summary of this thoughts in Philippians 4:11-13, "[11] I am not saying this because I am in need, for I have learned to be content whatever the circumstances. [12] I know what it is to be in need, and I know what it is to have plenty. I have learned the secret of being content in any and every situation, whether well fed or hungry, whether living in plenty or in want. [13] I can do all this through him who gives me strength."

Paul shares some dire warnings about loving money in I Timothy 6:9-10, "[9] Those who want to get rich fall into temptation and a trap and into many foolish and harmful desires that plunge people into ruin and destruction. [10] For the love of money is a root of all kinds of evil. Some people, eager for money, have wandered from the faith and pierced themselves with many griefs." It is not money itself that is evil, it is *loving* money.

When a person loves money, it is a beast with an insatiable thirst which can never be quenched. It causes a person to hoard money, utilize it for manipulation and control, and relentlessly pursue it regardless of the price it exacts on their relationships with others and the Lord. They refuse to be generous or share with others who are in need.

Thankfully, Paul shares insight into how to find contentment as he continued in I Timothy 6:11, "But you, man of God, flee from all this, and pursue righteousness, godliness, faith, love, endurance and gentleness." By pursuing these virtues, we can guard our hearts from being overtaken by greed, envy, and jealousy.

Paul eloquently summarizes his thoughts in I Timothy 6:17-19, "¹⁷ Command those who are rich in this present world not to be arrogant nor to put their hope in wealth, which is so uncertain, but to put their hope in God, who richly provides us with everything for our enjoyment. ¹⁸ Command them to do good, to be rich in good deeds, and to be generous and willing to share. ¹⁹ In this way they will lay up treasure for themselves as a firm foundation for the coming age, so that they may take hold of the life that is truly life."

There are two don'ts and five do's in Paul's summary:
- **Don't:** be arrogant
- **Don't:** put your hope in wealth; it is uncertain
- **Do:** put your hope in God
- **Do:** good
- **Do:** be rich in good deeds
- **Do:** be generous
- **Do:** be willing to share.

If you put this wisdom into practice in our life, it will help you gain contentment in all things and utilize financial resources in a God-honoring way. This will allow you to experience a type of peace only he can provide.

Summary: Sustaining Progress Toward Your Fully Funded Life

Let's look at all of the tips for sustaining progress toward your Fully Funded Life:

1. *Receive negative words as a challenge instead of a putdown.*
2. *Surround yourself with positive and encouraging people.*
3. *Write down your dream. Look at your dream. Review your dream.*
4. *Track your net worth quarterly.*
5. *Allow financial mentors to speak into your life.*
6. *Build and fiercely protect financial margin.*
7. *Make your goals (and your progress toward funding them) visual.*
8. *Hold your dreams loosely.*
9. *Become debt-free.*
10. *Practice contentment continually.*

What do all of these tips have in common? They all require personal discipline. It takes discipline to disregard negative words and people. It takes discipline to surround yourself with positive people. It requires discipline to review your dreams and net worth on a regular basis. Meeting with mentors requires discipline. Protecting your savings account from crazy spending habits requires discipline. Unclenching your fist and holding your dreams with a loose hand requires continual discipline. Becoming and staying debt-free requires constant discipline.

It all boils down to discipline. It requires diligence. As we saw in Proverbs 21:5, "The plans of the diligent lead to profit…" This is great news for all believers because diligence and self-discipline result from self-control, one of the fruits of the Spirit. We see this in Galatians 5:22-23, "22 But the fruit of the Spirit is love, joy, peace, forbearance, kindness, goodness, faithfulness, 23 gentleness and self-control. Against such things there is no law."

Do you see it? Self-control is a fruit of the Spirit, and it is at the heart of personal discipline. I encourage you to pray for the Lord to activate this powerful gift in your life as you pursue the God-given desires of your heart.

You can do this!

11

THE POWER OF BELIEF

As you have read this book, I have no doubt that you have encountered a variety of emotions. Maybe you have felt excitement for the possibilities of your future, enthusiasm for accomplishing a dream, and motivation to pursue several dreams. You have probably experienced unpleasant feelings, like doubting whether it is even possible to make progress at all. You may have even been tempted to write off dreaming entirely due to past challenges you have faced.

I want to remind you that all of these feelings are normal. Whenever we are faced with a huge dream or task, it is easy to become overwhelmed and succumb to the pressures and stress that quickly rush over us.

Knowing this, I felt it would be helpful to end this book with some encouragement. Let me start by saying, "You can do this!" As Paul wrote to the Romans in Romans 8:31: "*If God is for us, who can be against us?*" If God gave you plans, hopes, and dreams, He is *for* you and your dreams! As you encounter challenges, remind yourself regularly of this fact and begin to look for ways he is moving on your behalf.

> If God gave you plans, hopes, and dreams,
> He is for you and for your dreams!

126

Writing this book has allowed me to reflect on my own plans, hopes, and dreams. I can't believe how many God has funded on my behalf. As I think about them, there have been obstacles to accomplishing each one. Not all of them have looked exactly as I imagined them. They have certainly not come to fruition like I believed they would, but I can say unequivocally that God has been my Great Provider every step of the way.

One particular dream I had was to own a larger tract of land, to hike, hunt, and enjoy the beauty of God's great creation. I grew up on a farm and was able to roam freely through the fields and forests. Years later, I found myself living in a subdivision in a city. One day, I was driving to a speaking event to teach a Financial Learning Experience, and my mind was focused on this dream of owning a farm. The challenges to achieving my dream were more than I could really bear. Over the course of the four-hour car ride to my destination, my conversation with God became an excellent pity-party. "I'm never going to be able to own land," I said out loud. I continued with an endless thought pattern that went something like this: "This dream is never going to happen. It is too expensive. I'm always going to have to ask other people to let me hunt and explore their land. It would be easier to just give up on my dream and focus on something more realistic."

This was in 2009, and Jenn and I had just absorbed some terrible blows to some big dreams in our life. After nine years of infertility, we had unsuccessfully attempted IVF treatments. Our fixer-upper house had experienced one terrible disaster after another including failure of both heat pumps, a broken hot water heater, a complete roof replacement on the back of the house, and removal and replacement of all the sheet rock on the lower level. To add to our financial stress, we had stepped off staff at our church to pursue the I Was Broke. Now I'm Not. dream full-time.

Put lightly, the dream of owning any land seemed impossible. It was in the midst of grieving and throwing one of the best pity-parties you've ever seen that I felt God speak to me. As I pulled into a parking spot at my destination, this is what I sensed the Lord ask: "Joe, you have driven for the past four hours, and what was on both sides of the road?" It seemed like a rhetorical question, but I answered anyway, "Land. There was land on both sides of the road."

"That's right, Joe, and guess what? Someone owns *all* of it. I gave them the ability to own it. Don't you believe I could do the same for you?" Talk about a wake-up call! But then I felt God challenge me, "But you aren't preparing for the blessing. You have nothing saved for your dream. You aren't even looking at land. If a great deal on land came available right now for just $5,000, you probably wouldn't even know about it. Even if you did know about it, you are not in the financial position to purchase it. Prepare for the blessing as if you know it is coming and trust me to provide the opportunity."

With this word, I gained something that is perhaps the most powerful and valuable thing a person could possibly have—belief that God knew my dream. In that moment, I more fully understood what David meant when he wrote in Psalm 37:4: *"Take delight in the Lord, and he will give you the desires of your heart."* I had belief that God was going before me preparing the way. I was particularly *fired up* for the Financial Learning Experience I taught that evening! I knew my dream was on the way to becoming reality. In spite of the challenges we had faced, the dream was going to be connected to dollars. Stated another way: I had 20/20 vision!

Just a few months later, we learned the amazing news that God had worked a miracle, and we were pregnant with a baby boy!

He was born in February 2010, and later that year, guess what happened? A real estate agent who had heard about my dream approached me about a farm being sold at a steep discount due to the recession. As I inked the contract that made us the proud owners of a 68.605-acre farm, I felt as if God was winking at me as I recalled my pity-party from 18 months earlier.

To this day, every time I drive onto the farm, and especially when my son is with me, I am reminded that God still works miracles. I am literally taking my miracle son with me onto the miracle land.

The Belief Bank

I am no different than you. God loves you just like he loves me. The best way I can explain the power of belief is through something I call a "belief bank." This belief bank receives deposits and experiences withdrawals. Every time progress is made toward a dream, it places a deposit in your belief bank. Whenever a setback is experienced, we can withdraw some belief to pick ourselves up to continue pursuing the dream.

God has done so much for me that my belief bank is chock full of deposits. If your belief bank is empty, borrow some belief from me — interest free. Take some time today to seek him and listen to what he has to say to you. You will leave the conversation knowing God is for you, he is with you, and you can do whatever he has placed in your heart to do.

The Bible is full of great stories that should help fill our belief bank accounts. Moses crossed the sea on dry land. Joshua did the same, except he crossed a river (during flood season!) instead of a sea. David killed Goliath. Jonah survived three days in a giant fish. Noah survived 40 days of a worldwide rainfall and more than a year floating in a giant ship he had built before rain had ever fallen on the earth. At the words of Jesus, a paralyzed man walked away, Peter walked on water, and a man with a shriveled hand was made whole. Jesus overcame the cross and death itself. He is still in the miracle-working business! Believe it. Live your life knowing he is preparing the way and is for the dreams he has given you.

When he performs the miracle, be certain to give him all the praise and all of the glory. One of the primary reasons God makes some dreams seem impossible to us in our human minds is because it is a way for us to make him known to those that are far from him. Think about it: when a dream comes true that is lavish, undeserved, or unmerited, others around you will say, "How did this happen? It is impossible! I know you. This is simply not possible!" Moments like this will provide you the opportunity to say, "I know how it happened. It was impossible for me, but with God all things are possible. Let me tell you what the Lord has done for me!"

It is through our testimony that we become overcomers. As it is shared in Revelation 12:11: "They triumphed over him by the blood of the Lamb and by the word of their testimony." Embrace the challenges. Believe God will do what he has promised. Praise him when each dream becomes reality and freely share your belief with others as your belief bank overflows.

You have a 20/20 vision for your life. You've prepared a plan to fund each plan, hope, and dream. Chase each one with fervent energy and always know and believe this truth: you can do this. Go live your Fully Funded Life!

References and Footnotes

i http://www.oprah.com/money/oprahs-debt-diet-step-8/1

ii https://www.dictionary.com/browse/renew

iii https://www.newsweek.com/missing-cut-382954

iv https://www.psychologytoday.com/us/blog/the-moment-youth/201803/goal-setting-is-linked-higher-achievement

v Fran Tarkenton and Tiger Woods, Incredible Kid story: https://youtu.be/kfTY5xUFaJs

vi Bill and Melinda Gates Foundation https://www.gatesfoundation.org/

vii *Positioning Yourself to Prosper*, "Abraham's Lesson" – Lesson 2, Part 7, as developed and delivered by Bishop T. D. Jakes

viii https://knowledge.wharton.upenn.edu/article/the-retirement-problem-what-will-you-do-with-all-that-time/

ix "You Asked: Do Religious People Live Longer" http://time.com/5159848/do-religious-people-live-longer/

x "Not Done Dave's Way" https://www.daveramsey.com/askdave/other/not-done-daves-way

xi Ronald Wayne, Apple Computer https://en.wikipedia.org/wiki/Ronald_Wayne

xii Mike Markkula, Apple Computer https://en.wikipedia.org/wiki/Mike_Markkula

xiii Pebble Time Watch, Kickstarter Project https://www.kickstarter.com/projects/getpebble/pebble-time-awesome-smartwatch-no-compromises?ref=discovery_most_funded

xiv The Compound Annual Growth Rate of S&P 500, including dividends, from January 1941 through December 2017 - http://www.moneychimp.com/features/market_cagr.htm

xv 5% down payment of $17,500 and conventional mortgage with the following terms: 4.50% interest for 360 months – standard amortization

xvi *Rich Dad. Poor Dad.* By Robert Kiyosaki, https://www.knowledgebringsmoney.com/robert-kiyosaki.html

xvii Rep. Elijah Cummings speech during House Oversight and Government Reform meeting, February 27, 2019, https://www.youtube.com/watch?v=72gy-LZ4UN0&t=9s – Specific quote begins at 2:29

xviii Steve Harvey shares about his childhood television dream: https://www.youtube.com/watch?v=LqNRRLHaT0w